HEBREWS – A

# – HEBREWS –
## A THEMATIC STUDY

W. F. BARLING

THE CHRISTADELPHIAN
404 SHAFTMOOR LANE
HALL GREEN, BIRMINGHAM
B28 8SZ (UK)

2012

First published 2012

ISBN 978-0-85189-198-9

© 2012 The Christadelphian Magazine and Publishing Association Limited

*Printed and bound in Malta by:*
GUTENBERG PRESS LTD

# PREFACE

IF a project is not to be abandoned for lack of time to carry it out with the thoroughness which conscience demands, there is but one thing to do – to see it through to the utmost of one's ability in the limited time available. Such has been the case with these notes. Written in a race against the clock, they are the best that could be produced under difficult conditions. It is hoped therefore, that they will be read with a certain tolerance by those who were not present when the lectures, of which they record the substance, were given. Yet, in expressing that hope, the author has no wish to spare his work that searching scrutiny to which other students of the epistle have every right to submit it, the more so as the lectures were the fruit of much study on his part and also presupposed considerable familiarity with the text of Hebrews on the part of his listeners. Apart from other failings, one weakness such a work as this inevitably must have is that inherent in a thematic study. An analytical study has the drawback that it can all too easily blur for the reader the clear outlines of the epistle; a thematic study, on the other hand, can just as easily disconcert the reader by its rapid shuttling to and fro, and leave much of the epistle altogether unexplained, or, at best, only half explained. However, should the notes serve in any way to elucidate the epistle, and thus help some to appreciate better the privileges and responsibilities of the Christian calling, the labour to which the author and his faithful helpers have put themselves will have been amply rewarded.

W. F. BARLING<br>December, 1954

# FOREWORD

IN the early 1950s a series of weekly classes known as The London Bible Class were held during the autumn, usually in the St. Bride's Institute. Each year one speaker gave a series of studies, the late Brother Fred Barling being one of them.

During each address he would hold our attention without any apparent reference to notes. At the end, questions and comments would be invited and as these commenced, duplicated typed notes were circulated. We were astonished to find that the written notes of the paper we had just heard were virtually verbatim. It was a practice Brother Fred maintained throughout each of the series he took, even though he freely admitted the address for each evening had often only been completed during the days immediately before the class.

The printing of each week's material was aided by a small group of helpers, who then collated and bound full volumes at the end of each series. The books *Law and Grace* and *Jesus – Healer and Teacher* both began life this way, and this treatise on Hebrews is based on the Class notes of 1954.

Many speakers have different styles for speaking and writing and few can speak in a way that is acceptable in print. Brother Fred was an exception and one can read the words and almost relive the listening experience. There are relatively few of us now who will be able to recall those heady times, but hopefully with this volume a new generation will be able to appreciate the work of a brother who now rests, but whose enthusiasm for God's word and whose grasp of scripture lives on.

DEREK PALMER
September, 2012

# CONTENTS

| | | |
|---|---|---|
| | PREFACE | v |
| | FOREWORD | vi |
| 1 | "LET US HOLD FAST"<br>*The needs and circumstances of the readers* | 1 |
| 2 | "THINGS ... HARD TO BE UTTERED"<br>*The idiom and argumentation of the letter* | 26 |
| 3 | "HE SHALL BE TO ME A SON"<br>*The finality of the new revelation* | 44 |
| 4 | "THEM WHO DRAW BACK UNTO PERDITION"<br>*The fatal consequences of apostasy* | 57 |
| 5 | "FOR THE SUFFERING OF DEATH"<br>*The indispensability of the Cross* | 71 |
| 6 | "CROWNED WITH GLORY AND HONOUR"<br>*The Saviour exalted to priesthood* | 82 |
| 7 | "ONE SACRIFICE FOR SINS FOR EVER"<br>*The all-sufficiency of salvation through Christ* | 96 |
| 8 | "HE TAKETH AWAY THE FIRST"<br>*The Law repealed and replaced* | 112 |
| 9 | "GOD HAVING PROVIDED SOME BETTER THING"<br>*The need and secret of endurance* | 122 |
| 10 | "LET US GO FORTH THEREFORE UNTO HIM"<br>*The call to action and its relevance for today* | 136 |
| | SCRIPTURE REFERENCE INDEX | 153 |

# 1

## "LET US HOLD FAST"
*The needs and circumstances of the readers.*

WE set out to study what, in the Authorized Version of the Bible, is styled, "THE EPISTLE OF PAUL THE APOSTLE TO THE HEBREWS". This traditional title is categorical. It boldly affirms:

(a) that the work is to be classified as an epistle;
(b) that it was written by Paul;
(c) that it was despatched to readers of exclusively Jewish extraction.

The first of these affirmations is expressly authenticated by the text. The author himself refers to his work as "a letter" (13:22). This is in no way surprising: the tone of the work is throughout so personal, and its mode of address so frank and direct, that no other designation is conceivable. Were it in fact to lack the confirmation of the author, its aptness could not be called in question: in such an event, what he had failed to assert, we should be obliged to deduce for ourselves and to state on his behalf.

**The problem of authorship**

Such is far from being the case with regard to the second affirmation. For not only is there no mention made in the epistle of the author by name, but also such clues as to his identity as are there provided are too meagre and inconclusive to justify dogmatism, even when tradition is called to its aid. There is moreover a sound reason why we should not concern ourselves with the problem of authorship in a study whose sole aim is a right understanding of the meaning and message of the letter. Barely, if at all, would assurance as to the author's name elucidate for us his meaning in certain difficult passages. The fact is that even were the original manuscript to come to light tomorrow, with the author's signature upon it, our understanding of the epistle would in no material way be furthered. Our curiosity indeed would be satisfied, but that would be practically all. We shall here therefore respect the author's anonymity: for us he will remain just 'the author', 'the writer', or 'the sender' of the letter.

## The readers' identity

What, then, of the third affirmation made in the traditional title? For the fact has to be faced that if the writer goes unnamed, so do his readers. That would seem reason sufficient for not attempting to identify them either.

Two important factors, however, justify the attempt in their case, making it, if not actually imperative, at least highly desirable. The first of these is that tradition (whose value ought never to be lightly set aside) has not wavered over the readers' identity to anything like the extent that it has over the writer's. The designation "to the Hebrews" has never been seriously challenged, as has the ascription of the authorship to "Paul the Apostle". The second factor – doubly important because it explains the first – is that this designation is, in any case, in manifest keeping with the subject matter of the letter. Indeed, to be neutral on this issue is in practice impossible, for the very endeavour to read the epistle with true understanding forces a decision upon us. The same criterion which on the one hand excuses us from pronouncing on the matter of authorship, obliges us on the other to concern ourselves with the circumstances and estate – and so with the identity – of those who first received the letter. The effect is that, at several points, our interpretation of the text is conditioned by the conclusions which we have reached concerning these other debatable matters.

There is obvious danger in this: a false identification can mislead us, perhaps disastrously. That need not daunt us however since the converse is equally true, and the advantages to be gained by reaching a sound decision warrant the risks involved. Provided the greatest caution and prudence are exercised, we can therefore make an accurate identification our first objective, and with that end in view we shall now at once undertake a careful reconnaissance of the epistle as a whole.

## An overview of the letter

Our course is largely plotted for us in advance by the work itself, provided we take the writer absolutely at his word when he calls it "a letter". For what is a letter? In the very nature of things it is a communication about matters assumed by the writer to be of as great an interest or concern to his reader (or readers) as to himself. Its tone, its emphasis, the topics with which it deals, are thus each, in their special way, revelatory, serving as so many clues to the interests, the needs, and the circumstances of the correspondents in question. Thus where a letter to a group of people is found to abound in most solemn cautions, reinforced by the weightiest sanctions, we have every ground for concluding, on the one hand that the members of this group were contemplating some decisive change in their mode of life and thought, and on the other that the writer felt compelled to discourage them from the course of action in question because in his view it was of the gravest peril to them.

Now such is precisely the case with Hebrews. We find the writer repeatedly urging his readers to retain their hope and confidence – so their faith must have been faltering alarmingly; to rouse themselves to high endeavour, and shake off the hindrances of sloth – so he must have adjudged their zeal and effort wholly insufficient; to manifest afresh that courage which once won them such great renown lest they do themselves some irreparable harm – so their resolution must have been well nigh lost in the face of some sore trial which had befallen them and might well overwhelm them.

All this is legitimate inference. In brief, for the writer of Hebrews, a calamity assailed his readers from which he was determined by every means in his power to save them, ere it was too late. Had it been in fact too late to appeal to them, or were there actually no calamity impending, the letter would never have taken its existing form, or sounded such a note of deep concern. Warning and encouragement – both alike expressed in language instinct with passion – alternate throughout. The letter pulsates with a sense of crisis, and the writer is manifestly straining his powers of persuasion to save his readers from what he considers to be an act of spiritual suicide. To the very end, he cannot be sure of having won them over to his point of view and is thus constrained to end with the tender plea:

"I beseech you, brethren, suffer the word of exhortation: for I have written a letter unto you in few words." (13:22)

## The apology for brevity

The apology for brevity which reinforces the plea is full of significance for us, for it embraces, we note, the entire epistle in its scope: it envisages not some particular section, or sections, of the letter but rather the whole of it. Now, given the atmosphere of crisis and of tension which throughout characterizes the epistle, we can be confident that only when the writer felt certain that he had written enough to ensure the achievement of his purpose – when he was convinced, that is, that he had dealt with *all* his readers' difficulties – would he have ventured to bring his letter to a close. To omit any argument, any single point, essential to his purpose, he would not have dared: he would have deemed it a dereliction of most solemn duty. Yet, on the other hand, how lame would his apology for brevity have sounded, if his care to omit nothing vital had not been matched by a corresponding care to admit into the letter only what was strictly germane to its purpose and directly contributory to its success. To have excluded, for example, a discussion of so important a topic as the typical significance of the sacred furnishings of the Tabernacle on the plea of lack of time (9:5), and yet to have included the discussion of trivial or unimportant matters, would have been not only foolish and insincere, but also downright criminal.

The writer is manifestly too capable a logician, and too manifestly in earnest, for us to suspect him capable of such a fault; and the conclusion is forced upon us that everything in the letter, every single topic treated, was conceived by him as contributing to his overriding polemical purpose however unrelated it might at first seem to us to be. This means that every discussion had a close bearing upon the situation of his readers at the time – upon their fears, their doubts, their inclinations and their needs. We need constantly to realize this, to realize that it was the same passion and the same crisis which inspired the calmer and more formal portions of the epistle as the more emotional and personal sections, and that both are of equal evidential value for us in our search for clues, firstly as to the nature of the crisis presupposed in the epistle, and secondly as to the identity and circumstances of those who were confronted by it. If we so regard them we find that the letter abounds in information concerning the readers, and that inference can be much safer a guide to us here than would at first seem possible.

What then, looking either directly or obliquely at the epistle, do we find it telling us about these important matters?

**Addressed to Christians**

To state that the readers were Christians is almost superfluous. The epistle would not otherwise have been admitted into the New Testament canon. It is sufficient merely to skim the epistle with the eye to catch references to the Lord on every hand, and the simplest fact to establish is that those to whom the epistle was despatched had made a profession of faith in Jesus.

They had done so a full generation before. Several factors bear this out. They had been converted by the immediate disciples of the Lord who are spoken of with an air of remoteness which presupposes a considerable lapse of time (2:4). The same is true also of the way in which the writer has to remind his readers of the endurance which they had shown under trial in their early days as Christians (10:32). In addition, he is justified in sternly rebuking their lack of understanding because they have had time enough by now to attain to spiritual maturity (5:12-14). The tragedy is that the passage of time has not strengthened their faith but, on account of their neglect, has rather weakened it, and left them wholly unprepared for the new trial which has come upon them. They are tempted to desert Christ (2:3; 10:29). Full of alarm, the author hastens to save them from such ruinous folly. Repeatedly he counsels steadfastness and perseverance in the Faith. "We are made partakers of Christ", says he, "if we hold the beginning of our confidence stedfast unto the end" (3:14). His advice to them is:

> "Let us run with patience the race that is set before us, looking unto Jesus the author and finisher of our faith ... Consider him ... lest ye be wearied and faint in your minds." (12:1-3)

## A distinctive group

In so exhorting them, in these general terms, the author might well have been writing to any or all of the early Christian communities whose loyalty to Jesus was being put to some sore test. His choice of language in these particular passages tells us no more about his readers than that their Christian faith and resolution had grown weak. But in that respect it is not typical. In other passages a wholly distinctive note can be caught, for, in these, precisely the same advice is tendered in quite different terms, in language which transports us into a world fundamentally different from our own. It is in them — and they are in a decided majority — that the authentic note of the epistle is struck. Here is what is, perhaps, the most distinctive of them of all, dense in its thought, rich in its allusions, and consequently obscure for us today unless we familiarise ourselves with its characteristic idiom:

"For it is a good thing that the heart be established with grace; not with meats, which have not profited them that have been occupied therein. We have an altar, whereof they have no right to eat which serve the tabernacle. For the bodies of those beasts, whose blood is brought into the sanctuary by the high priest for sin, are burned without the camp. Wherefore Jesus also, that he might sanctify the people with his own blood, suffered without the gate. Let us go forth therefore unto him without the camp, bearing his reproach. For here have we no continuing city, but we seek one to come. By him therefore let us offer the sacrifice of praise to God continually, that is, the fruit of our lips giving thanks to his name." (13:9-15)

## Jewish Christians

If other passages in the epistle can be regarded as appropriate to the needs of all classes of Christians undergoing trial, this one certainly cannot be. It at once marks out the Christians to whom it was addressed as constituting a distinctive group, with needs and interests all their own. It plunges us not so much into the world of two thousand, as of more than three thousand years ago. It is not only to the dawn of the Christian dispensation that we are carried back, but also far beyond that to the very dawn of the Mosaic age. If the mention of a city and a city gate suggests a settled urban community of first century days, we also find ourselves on the march through the wilderness with the Twelve Tribes of Israel, with the sacred Tabernacle in their midst, and their eyes set on the Promised Land. In a brief compass we have to do with dietetic regulations; with sacrifice upon the holy Altar, and in particular with the chiefest offerings of all, the special Sin Offerings of the Day of Atonement; with the manipulation of blood in conformity with the detailed liturgical regulations laid down in Leviticus; with the Sanctuary and with the duties and privileges of the priests and High Priest therein – in brief with a whole array of topics of anything but universal interest, recounted or alluded to so summarily, and in such rapid succession, that the writer clearly assumes his readers to be both fully informed on these specialist matters, and capable in consequence of seizing the point of his remarks.

When read only cursorily, therefore, the passage tells us that it envisages a Christian community of a peculiar character, one intimately familiar with, if not actually engrossed with, the ceremonial observances of the Law of Moses. So true is this that, strangely enough, to convince his readers that such observances are now no longer valid the writer finds himself obliged to present his arguments actually in terms of those observances! The conclusion is inescapable. These men were not only Christians but also *Jews*; Jews steeped in their age-old Law, fondly attached to it, zealous guardians of it, needing to be convinced that its prescriptions were now no longer valid, but could – and should – be dispensed with utterly, to give place to the worship of God in spirit and in truth. To no category of Christians would the writer need to be at such pains to demonstrate the superiority of Christ to Moses, or to prove the necessity and fitness of the Cross, but to those for whom the Law of Moses was the pre-eminent divine revelation, and for whom the very notion of a crucified Messiah was a scandal and a stumblingblock – in a word, to Christians who were also Jews to the core.

**Appealing to the Old Testament**

The discussion of these capital themes in the letter is not coldly academical, but throbs with passion, precisely because for the readers, as Jews, so much was at stake. That is why the opening words of the epistle presuppose readers with as great an interest in what God revealed in times past through the prophets as, in what He had of late revealed through His Son; why all the warnings in the letter, from first to last, assume a profound reverence on the part of the recipients for the word spoken by angels at Sinai; why appeal is everywhere made to the Old Testament, and the Old Testament alone; and why the entire argumentation of the epistle is designed to establish the superiority of the new Christian order to the old Mosaic dispensation.

For any group of believers who were Jews, as well as Christians, the crisis of choice presupposed in the epistle was bound to arise. There were portents of it in the controversies between Jesus and the Pharisees. The issue held fire for so long after the Day of Pentecost only because the converts made during that time were without exception Jews, and because the whole Christian community in Jerusalem was content to remain strictly orthodox in its religious practices, even though it was unorthodox in its fundamental article of faith. To suggest that the situation should ever be otherwise embroiled Stephen with the Jewish authorities, and for his vision and courage in declaring that a new age had dawned with the preaching of the Gospel, and that both Law and Temple had now been rendered obsolete, he was made to pay with his blood (Acts 6–7).

## Division between Jewish and Gentile converts

The persecution which his adversaries forthwith directed against his fellow Jewish Christians quenched for a time any desire which some of these might have felt to adopt his point of view – let alone to apply, and proclaim it. But, in the providence of God, it was this same persecution, nonetheless, which largely served by its consequences to awaken the infant church to the realization of its true duty. It prepared the believers at Jerusalem for the shock of the conversion of Cornelius, and led at Antioch to the preaching of the Gospel not only to proselytes or half-proselytes like Cornelius, but even to full pagans owning no allegiance to the Jewish faith (Acts 10–11). Within a brief time Gentiles began to flow into the Church in ever increasing numbers, and mixed assemblies of Jewish Christians with centuries of Old Testament tradition behind them, and of Gentile Christians endowed for the most part with only an utterly worthless religious heritage, became a commonplace.

The immediate result was a crisis within the Church which almost spelt disaster (Acts 15). This revolution – for such it was – made the Law of Moses – its authority, its validity, its continued observance – a burning issue for every mixed assembly. How did these Gentile converts stand? They, to whose life and experience the prescriptions of the Law were so foreign, could they be regarded as authentic Christians unless they, like their Jewish brethren, became obedient to those prescriptions? A conflict of opinion arose, and scarcely a church escaped the ravages of the dispute. Echoes of the controversy still resound for us in Galatians, in 1 and 2 Corinthians, in Romans, and elsewhere.

**Addressed to Jews**

In this respect the kinship between those epistles and Hebrews is very close, and on grounds of subject matter it at first seems logical to class it with them. But this, in fact, we cannot do. Its special features forbid it. It never so much as alludes to circumcision. Unlike these other epistles, far from aiming to demonstrate the discontinuity between the New and the Old, it strives to emphasize their essential harmony as successive stages in one and the same purposive scheme of revelation. It never, like them, talks now in an idiom or in imagery peculiarly suited to Gentiles, now in language of special aptness for Jewish saints.[1] Its treatment is uniform, throughout adapted to a fixed point of view – the traditionally Jewish. This can only mean that it was addressed to a community which was Jewish to a man, one in which the propriety of circumcision needed no discussion precisely because all were the subjects of it, and practised it, as a matter of course.

Let this general conclusion be adopted and several minor features of the epistle at once assume a new and arresting significance. We see, for example, that those to whom God spoke in the past by the prophets, are

---
1. Note, for example, the similarity of idea, but the striking difference of treatment, to be found between 1 Corinthians 9:24-27 and 10:1-12.

styled "the fathers" (1:1; 3:9) not capriciously, but with real aptness, because "fathers" they quite literally were to all Jews, believing and unbelieving alike (cf. "Your fathers" in the quotation of Psalm 95 in 3:9). Even more striking is the fact that, to demonstrate the Saviour's oneness with mankind, the writer should contrast the nature of angels not with that of men in general, but with that of Jews in particular:

> "For verily he took not on him the nature of angels; but he took on him the *seed of Abraham.*" (2:16)

This, which would otherwise strike us as an outlandish way of expressing a momentous truth of universal interest, wins our admiration for the author's polemical skill and timely tact once we see him to be offsetting the stubborn prejudice of *Jews*, and striving the better to dispose them to accept the implications of the Lord's humanity by showing Jesus to have been "made like unto his brethren" even to the point of being born of their own ethnic stock (verse 17).

## A New Covenant

This same careful choice of words is likewise to be observed in the discussion of the New Covenant foretold by Jeremiah. In the prophet's day more than half the chosen people had already been in exile for over a century, and it was his sad task to announce that the remainder were soon to follow them. But he had also good news to bring. God, said Jeremiah, would one day reverse His work of judgement, and this not only for the house of Judah but also for the house of Israel. Both divisions of the nation would eventually find favour with God and be restored to their land.

> "Behold, the days come, saith the LORD, that I will make a new covenant with the house of Israel, and with the house of Judah." (Jeremiah 31:31)

The writer of Hebrews lifts these words bodily out of the book of Jeremiah, and builds an argument upon them. It is an argument, be it noted, with a special preoccupation – a preoccupation with the *newness* of the covenant foretold by the prophet (Hebrews 8:8-

13). This newness was of major concern to Jeremiah himself also, but for obvious reasons, the fact that the New Covenant was to be made with precisely the *same* people as the Old was also of capital importance for him. This, interestingly enough, is left quite unstressed in the epistle – so much so that, in our concern to follow the course of the argument, we easily fail to note the fact. Yet, when we think upon the matter, it is obvious that had Hebrews been addressed to a mixed church, for the Gentile contingent the argument would have been lacking in point, unless some explanation had also been given of the means whereby blessings guaranteed expressly to Jews after the flesh became valid also for those who belonged by birth neither to the house of Israel nor to the house of Judah. Now no such explanation is furnished in Hebrews. This must mean either that the author was guilty of an unpardonable omission, or that he had no need to furnish an explanation because no need existed for it, the group in question being made up exclusively of Jews. It is obvious which way we must choose. The truth is that, because the writer was dealing only with men proud of their Abrahamic ancestry, it served his purpose admirably to quote against them promises which were only strictly relevant for such as they. It was only to men belonging to the race to which both Covenants were made that the application of the terms "first" and "old" to the one, and of "second" and "new" to the other, could come home with the force intended by the writer or, indeed, have any pertinence whatever.

## Allusions to the Law

The same evidential value attaches, as we have already seen, in part, to the great themes of the epistle. There is not the slightest mention anywhere of any alternative to the priesthood of Christ but that of Aaron, or of any earthly sanctuary other than that pitched by Moses in the wilderness. At the very heart of the writer's argument concerning sacrifice lies the imposing ritual of what was for the Jews – *but only for the Jews* – the day of days. With his mind so full of the significant ritual of that Day he can take a characteristic leap in thought, and talk, as we saw above, of Jesus suffering without the gate, "that he might sanctify the people", yet feel no need either to define his terms, or to specify which "people" it is that he has in mind. For him it would manifestly be superfluous to do either the one or other, the more so because here, as everywhere else in the epistle, only one people have any importance both for him and for his readers – to wit, the chosen race (cf. 2:17; 5:3; 7:5, etc.). Likewise, of only one possible alternative form of worship to the Christian – that is, the out-and-out Mosaic – is any account whatsoever taken.

It is this which of course explains, and excuses, the repeated use of liturgical imagery which would mean so little to former pagans – phrases such as, "when he had by himself purged our sins" ... "having our hearts sprinkled", and the like. Such language, which would merely have sown confusion for a mixed community, would, on the contrary, for a group consisting exclusively of Jews, have sounded natural, normal and appealing. Realizing this, we can the better understand why the writer chose to couch even his crucial concluding appeal in the same allusive idiom. "Let us go forth therefore unto him", said he, "without the camp, bearing his reproach". Manifestly, only those who were, on grounds of race, automatically members of the camp, and anxiously desirous to remain so, could be properly called upon to leave it by such an act of solemn choice.

Enough: the point need be pressed no further. These readers were, beyond all cavil, Jews, and our epistle is only too rightly styled the letter "to the *Hebrews*".

## Replacing the Law and its practices

That matter finally settled, let us now endeavour to ascertain what were their intellectual and moral difficulties and thus arrive, if possible, at the stage where we can with confidence identify them as a group.

Here the point must be made afresh that the range of topics discussed in the epistle provides us with a mass of circumstantial detail concerning its original recipients as is the case with all the other New Testament letters. But, as we have seen, what marks Hebrews off so sharply from each of these is the highly specialist nature of its themes. The writer here is not, like those other writers, intent on giving reasons why the Gentile element in the church should be exempted from the observance of the Law, or seeking to settle the thorny problems of religious conscience peculiar to a mixed assembly of Gentiles and Jews. He handles far more explosive matters. He sets out to convince actual Jews, long accustomed by habit to think it their sacred duty to continue to practise that observance, that it is now no longer legitimate for them to do so! Well might we admire his courage, the more so as he undertakes this task in the full knowledge that, if he succeeds, the effects of his reasoning will not be confined to his purely Christian readers. It is bound to have repercussions also, similar to those of Stephen's day, among the non-Christian Jews among whom those readers live and worship. These men cannot be expected to content themselves with disowning Christian Jews as Jews. It is also a foregone conclusion that they will heap ostracism upon them, and add to that not only the confiscation of their goods but also imprisonment, maltreatment and maybe death itself. Yet by all this our writer is unmoved. So convinced is he of the rightness of his cause, that he crowns his epistle with the astounding call to his readers to take the initiative in this matter. He bids them effect the breach with Jewry, boldly and of their own accord, taking Jesus himself as their example in despising the shame, and in bearing the reproach, which will inevitably fall upon them for so doing.

Thus reviewing the epistle, we come to appreciate that from the very outset the writer labours under a grievous handicap. He has to bring about an intellectual conviction so strong that it will win consent for the drastic step which now he deems essential and overdue. He is plainly aware – the tenseness of atmosphere in the epistle is witness – that this attempt of his is a unique opportunity, as it is his one and only means of ensuring that that step is taken, and that upon the success or failure of this one vital communication depends the whole fate of his Jewish readers as *Christians*. Either, as a result, they will "go on" to perfection, or they will instead "draw back" – and that to perdition.

Decision of one kind or other there must be. They have manifestly been confronted with a straight choice between Christ and Moses. The danger is indeed great that they will turn traitors to the one both out of traditional regard for the other and out of fear of their fellows. He counters that temptation by bidding them remain loyal to Christ, regardless of the consequences in terms of suffering and sacrifice, whether mental or physical. What makes his task so especially difficult is that all along he has to contend against the settled conviction in their minds that their Law, because ordained by God at Sinai, is immutable, valid for all time, absolutely binding upon them as literal, physical, children of the Covenant. Never, if he is to succeed in his delicate undertaking, must he even appear to impugn the divine authority of that Law. Yet, while upholding and glorifying it – as they do themselves – he must also somehow lead them to the distasteful conclusion that their belief in its continued validity is a fatal fallacy utterly subversive of the new faith which once they were so proud and bold to profess.

At no stage dare he risk a false step: yet at no stage, either, must he miss any opportunity of disposing their minds and hearts to accept that staggering call with which he knows he must conclude, repugnant though it will assuredly be to them. Gone for all time, all too obviously, are the tranquil days of compromise, days in which they have been placidly content to ally their profession of faith in Christ to an uncritical traditional observance of the Law of Moses, and have neglected to prepare themselves for the crisis which, sooner or later, was bound to come.

THE LETTER TO THE HEBREWS
## The readers' location
Where, we have reason to ask, could circumstances thus arise, in which a group of Jewish Christians could, on this particular issue, be presented with this awful choice of falling either into the hands of men or into the hands of God? To ask is to answer. In no city of the Roman world would the orthodox Jewish authorities have either the right or the audacity to present their Christian brethren with this choice. Only in Palestine itself could such a situation possibly come about.

Does our epistle presuppose, then, as this fact would lead us to expect, that the readers were Palestinians? The text gives several significant hints to that effect.

It is noteworthy that the author makes a point of proving that the settlement in Canaan under Joshua was not the attainment of the true Rest of God. Why should he bother to do so? True, his allegorical treatment of the wilderness journey in a sense necessitates it: if that journey is viewed as an allegory of the Christian life, then it follows that the settlement must also, in its turn, be viewed as a figure of the life to come. But what is remarkable is that the writer feels the obligation to *establish* his right so to regard the settlement. First we find him marshalling his Old Testament texts, next adding his explanatory comments, then, finally, appealing to his readers' common, sense, contending that, "If Jesus (i.e., Joshua) had given them rest, then would he not afterward have spoken of another day" (4:3-8). We can be sure that he does not go to such lengths without good reason, the more so as he drives home his point with a triumphant concluding deduction, implying that the fact had been seriously challenged – "There *remaineth* therefore a rest to the people of God". Since, then, he is refuting a contrary opinion, and doing so for Christians who are also zealous Jews, it is obvious what this particular opinion was. Certain were contending, or were at least disposed to believe, that the occupation of the Land was in actual fact the realization of the rest envisaged by God.

But of what burning interest would all this be to Jews resident in some large Roman city, and long habituated to absence from the Land? Effectively, none: the whole issue would be too abstract a concern for them to bother themselves sufficiently about it for a writer, so much in earnest, and so preoccupied with urgent matters, as the sender of this letter, to devote special time end attention to it. Such would not be the case, however, with Christian Jews, for whom Palestine was a permanent and hallowed homeland. Among them it would be normal to find some whose attachment to their Land was just as fervent as to their revered Law itself. Especially would this be true about a generation from the Lord's day, for the first mutterings could then already be heard of the Jewish War of Independence, in which out of zeal for the national cause, fanatical patriots would shortly choose to challenge the might of invincible Rome. Such men, we can be sure, in common with patriots of every other land and age, would have no sympathy for Christians who hesitated to throw their lot in with them, and whose faith in any case appeared in their eyes as the rankest heresy. They would assuredly put the sorest pressure upon their Christian compatriots and these, understandably, would tend to wilt before their threats and propaganda. Thus, let us but once see Hebrews as a counter to that pressure, as a message of succour to hard-pressed Palestinian Christians, tempted to forfeit their eternal salvation on the altar of mere earthly loyalties, and a flood of fresh light is thrown upon it.

This becomes particularly obvious in the eleventh chapter of the epistle, where the Land comes into view with the mention of Abraham. Abraham, says the writer, "when he was called to go out into a place which he should after receive for an inheritance, obeyed, and he went out, not knowing whither he went" (11:8). Not till the very end of the epistle will the readers consciously perceive the significance of this comment, or feel its impact to the full. Little do they at this stage realize the author's design, know that he is bearing them inexorably on towards a similar call to go out, to sever their own bonds with kith and kin as completely as did their illustrious forefather in ancient days.

But the fact remains – and so the writer has to take account of it – that the break brought Abraham in due course to the Land itself. Yet what was the attitude which even he, to whom it was personally promised, took up towards it? "By faith," says the writer, "he *sojourned* in the land of promise, *as in a strange country*" (11:9).

Is this comment made for its own sake, or with polemical design? If the former, we can have scant respect for the author. But if the latter – as must indeed be – we have reason to ask what was the design, and what the need, which called it forth. Let us but recognize it as offsetting the misplaced zeal of other residents in the Land, with a fundamentally different attitude to it from that of Abraham, and all becomes plain. The writer is then seen to be hinting, in the most convincing way, that the fact that the Land is the *Promised* Land is no reason why, in the new situation that has arisen, the Jewish Christians now living there should be so anxious to stand on their right to claim it as their national heritage. To counter the propaganda of the zealots, he holds up before them as authentic children of Abraham, only those who shared this pilgrim outlook with him – to wit, Isaac and Jacob who, though the "heirs with him of the same promise", were content like him to dwell in tents (verse 9). Their example, like their father's, should for the readers of the epistle serve as an invitation – an invitation to cultivate the same indifference to the claims of mere physical birth and purely national loyalties, and to adopt for themselves the same habit of regarding themselves as only temporary residents – *and even as actual foreigners* – in the Land, lawfully theirs though it was.

No clearer proof surely could be needed that the readers were themselves Palestinians. How wonderfully suited to their case, is the language, on that assumption.

And the same is true elsewhere. The precedent of Moses then becomes astoundingly relevant also; for, though Egypt was an alien land, for him it was nevertheless what Palestine was to these Christians – a *native* land. With the fortunes of its ruling house his own were intimately bound up. Yet he abjured these merely earthly attachments and by a decisive act of faith, he "forsook Egypt" – as shortly the writer is going to call upon his readers to forsake loyalty even to the Holy Land itself (11:24-27).

**"No continuing city"**

As the author composed his epistle and thus skilfully related it to his readers' mood and need, how anxiously he must have wondered whether they would make the same resolute choice as these men of old. They were products of their status as children of Abraham, and of the heritage which was theirs as such – and rightly so. But would they, he must have asked himself, see their duty set forth for them by their fierce compatriots, burning with misplaced patriotism, or by these illustrious Old Testament figures? Upon one thing he was resolved – that if a false choice there was to be, his would not be the responsibility for it, but theirs alone. For his part he would delicately, warily, manoeuvre them into a position of preparedness to do what otherwise they could never be constrained to do – formally cut themselves off from those with whom the ties of blood and religious culture were so strong, and in whose eyes they would seem to be guilty at once of sedition and of heresy in refusing to join the patriotic cause. His duty thus done, the onus would then be on them.

The call, when it came, was masterly. Phrase after phrase, as we shall be in a better position to judge later on, recalled and drove home all the previous carefully wrought doctrinal arguments, reinforced all the tactful hints let fall in passing. One phrase in particular – the final reason pleaded for obedience – threw the whole weight of the patriarchs' example into the balance. "Let us go forth therefore," says the writer, "unto him without the camp, bearing his reproach. For here have we no continuing city, but we seek one to come" (13:13,14).

This motive for action – "for here have we no continuing city" – as its very position is witness, was, in the writer's judgement, the crowning, clinching, factor. In it he pointedly recalled to them not only the example of faith which Abraham had set, but also the compelling reason which had motivated Abraham to act as he did. Reverting to the eleventh chapter once more, we find the writer saying that why Abraham chose to sojourn in the Land of Promise, as in a strange country, was because "he looked for a city which hath foundations, whose builder and maker is God" (11:10). Nor does he content himself with stating this fact once. He returns to the matter a little later, stressing first that those who have an outlook like the patriarchs "declare plainly that they seek a country". "*Seek*", we note. The word speaks volumes. It means that the patriarchs, even in the Land of Promise, still sought another! That is precisely what the author is presently going to ask his readers in turn to do. But how can they? By doing what the patriarchs did, by looking beyond all earthly lands to a transcendent reality unseen by the merely natural eye.

"Truly, if they had been mindful of that country from whence they came out, they might have had opportunity to have returned. But now they desire a better country, that is, an heavenly."      (11:15,16)

At this God was pleased, says the author, and gave practical proof of the fact in calling Himself at the bush by the name of Abraham, Isaac and Jacob, thus indicating His intention to grant them the object of their desire.

"Now they desire a better country, that is, an heavenly: wherefore God is not ashamed to be called their God for he hath prepared for them a city."      (verse 16)

There we have it once more – the mention of a *city*. The link between the concluding call in the thirteenth chapter, and the argumentation of the eleventh, is thus made doubly obvious. But this raises, rather than solves, a problem. With the respect for the author's polemical prowess which we have already had cause to feel, we may well wonder why the writer should so preoccupy himself with the topic of a "city". It does not suffice to note the verbal link: we must also discover its pertinence for the readers.

### Dwelling in Jerusalem

We have not far to seek. The fact that the epistle was composed to deal with the peculiar difficulties and temptations of a special community implies that the readers formed a fairly compact group. This is confirmed by the fact that the writer could contemplate paying them all a visit at the same time (13:19), and especially by the fact that he could speak of them as having a distinct body of spiritual leaders to whom it was their duty to show themselves submissive and obedient (13:7,17). It is therefore justifiable to regard them as living in or around one centre of population or, if, quite literally, they had by now "fled for refuge" from that centre (6:18), as remaining firmly attached to it and hoping to return there. That is, they are a group with a developed *civic* consciousness: the writer speaks so repeatedly of the subject of a city simply because the topic bulks so large in their minds and he finds it necessary to counter a definite preoccupation on their part with a certain city in particular. Both he and they would be fully aware which city that was, so that he would not need to go into detail concerning it but only to deal with their attachment to it. It would therefore be in keeping with his technique of argument to make only tactfully veiled allusions to it.

One of these leaps to the eye is in his momentous concluding call. If, instead of concerning ourselves with following the intricacies of the writer's thought, we pay heed to what we might term topographical data, we find that the passage reads thus:

"The bodies of those beasts ...
   are burned *without the camp*.
Wherefore Jesus suffered ...
   *without the gate*.
Let us go forth therefore unto him *without the camp* ...
   for here have we no continuing *city*".

It at once strikes our notice, when the verses are thus arranged, that the writer does not stop to specify outside precisely what gate Jesus suffered. Have we any need to enquire why? Is it not perfectly obvious that only readers coming from *inside* the gate could so casually be assumed to be familiar with the fact that it was *outside* it that the Lord was crucified? This is borne out also by the fact that, whereas in the first parallelism, "camp" and "gate" are used as matching terms, it is "camp" and "city" which are used in the second – clearly because the particular city which served to illustrate the general truth, "Here have we no continuing city", was none other than that outside whose gate Jesus was put to death as the antitypical Sin Offering. Jerusalem, then-Jerusalem the centre and embodiment of the entire religious system to which these Hebrews were so fondly and so mistakenly clinging – this was the city which prompted these pointed hints and allusions by the writer. First land, then city – such, together with the Law, were the objects of their love. To offset their attachment to the one the author had spoken of another country – to wit, "a *heavenly*" (11:16). What else can he be doing then, but offsetting their attachment to the other also when he tells them, "Ye are come unto mount Zion, and unto the city of the living God" and at once proceeds to define that city as "the *heavenly* Jerusalem, thus making the contrast with the earthly Jerusalem all the more explicit (12:22)?

## The imminent destruction of Jerusalem

We can now the better appreciate why, with pointed emphasis, he affirms, "for *here* have we no continuing city", and insists that they, as Christians, must "seek one *to come*" (13:14). He is, moreover, exploiting yet another of his earlier arguments here, for he has already demonstrated from the prophecy of Haggai the certain outcome of the imminent struggle with Rome (12:25-27) and is dispelling the fond illusions of his readers concerning their beloved city. Despite its glorious past, it is not invincible and indestructible as they imagine. Only the heavenly land and the heavenly city which were the objects of Abraham's hope will, in the coming convulsion, prove to be unshakeable and abiding. It is futile for them to imagine that the desperate defence of the earthly Jerusalem will stay the execution of the divine intention to bring it – and the outworn ceremonial worship of which it had been so long the glorious symbol – to ruin. Their duty is not to participate in the defence of either, but rather to reconcile themselves to inescapable facts.

"Wherefore [says he] we receiving a kingdom which cannot be moved, let us have grace, whereby we may serve God acceptably with reverence and godly fear: for our God is a consuming fire." (12:28,29)

There would clearly be no need thus to warn the readers to anticipate a national catastrophe unless that catastrophe were imminent, or to bid them not wantonly involve themselves in it, unless they were actually contemplating such a course of action. Such a catastrophe can only be identified, clearly, with the fall of Jerusalem in AD 70, and, with it, the ruin of the Temple and the formal closure of the Mosaic dispensation. This closure, when the epistle was written, had still to come about, for there were still priests that offered gifts according to the Law (8:4) and the divinely ordained dissolution had not yet become history (verse 13). And if further proof were needed of this fact, we have it, surely, in the note of urgency everywhere to be caught in the epistle. Had Jerusalem already been laid in ruins, and history had already proved the letter's thesis to be true, how gratuitous and far-removed from actuality would so much of its reasoning have sounded. But, as things were, how additionally timely, for example, the quotation of Jeremiah's promise of the inauguration of a new and better covenant would appear to the readers. For had not Jeremiah, too, lived in an age when Jerusalem and its Temple were likewise doomed to come to ruin, and preached a similar message of non-resistance? The readers, then, far from seeing in the contemporary political situation a call to participate in the defence of their ancient land and faith, were invited rather to behold the finger of God, working to effect the removal of an outworn religious system which, though indeed established by Him, had also now been superseded according to His own express will – a will revealed explicitly in the prophets and, enigmatically even in the Law itself. They were to face the fact that an epoch was drawing to its close before their eyes, as had another before the eyes of Jeremiah upon whose message now they were urged to place all their reliance.

**Suffering for their faith**

It was, however, a time which would demand the utmost courage of them. Jeremiah had been prepared to suffer for his faith – and did; did, what is more, in their own sacred city. Would they do likewise? To bring the readers to the point of saying, 'Yes', is everywhere the writer's aim, patent though it is only in the concluding chapters. As he knows only too well, a fateful choice lies before them; to choose as he would have them choose amounts in the eyes of their zealous unbelieving Jewish brethren to sympathy with the enemy and merits the severest punishment. Well might they quail, and unenviable indeed is their lot. But shall they proudly claim as natural heroes, and yet not be willing to emulate, those who, in times past, "were tortured, not accepting deliverance; that they might obtain a better resurrection"; or who "were stoned" and even "sawn asunder"; or who "wandered in deserts, and in mountains, and in dens and caves of the earth"? (11:35-38). This is language used, not for its own sake, but, like everything else in the epistle, used solely on account of its aptness, of its relation to the readers' needs and circumstances. They could so easily be lured into making Esau's choice and casting away their priceless spiritual heritage out of mere fear to suffer physically (12:16). They could, on the other hand, match Rahab's astuteness, have the vision to see in impending events the portents of their city's doom, as she in her day had foreseen the ruin of her own (11:31). What they needed to remember was that God is a *rewarder* of them that diligently seek him (verse 6) and that the essential thing to ensure was that, come what loss there might on earth, there would yet remain for them, "in heaven, a better and an enduring substance" (10:34).

## Preparing for the trial

It was with this end in view that the writer composed this momentous letter. He would do his utmost to put his hard-pressed readers on their guard against the insidious temptation to turn apostate to their glorious hope; he would strive with all the persuasiveness at his command to bid them lay aside every hindrance to fidelity – the Law included. They have much to make them hesitate. They feel lost and bewildered. The fault, moreover, is wholly theirs because they have failed to develop spiritually and so to realize the doctrinal and practical implications of their faith. The result is that they are woefully unprepared for the trial which has come. No matter, the writer will save them if he can, and comes, pen in hand, to their succour. He lists the points of scandal for the Jew in the new faith in Christ, resolves to deal manfully with them and also with the specious pretexts with which the waverers seek to justify the apostasy which they are so seriously contemplating. The result is this masterly "word of exhortation" which we, in this study, have made it our purpose, under the blessing of God, to understand and explain aright.

# 2

## "THINGS ... HARD TO BE UTTERED"
*The idiom and argumentation of the letter.*

IF the readers of Hebrews were Jewish there can be no doubt that the writer was also. The pregnant terms of his call, "Let us go forth ... without the camp", disclose not only their ancestry but his as well. Indeed, had he not been one of themselves never would he have been able to enter so sympathetically into their experience, or to give his message the form which he did. To study that form, and appreciate its distinctiveness, must be the next task we set ourselves.

**Tactful persuasion**
It emerges clearly early in the reading of the letter that the writer was determined to transform his readers' conception of both the nature and the role of their revered Law. He came to announce a change of dispensation – what he called "the time of reformation" (9:10). This, as we now well know, was indeed a delicate undertaking. He had to take every precaution not to offend in the process their tenderest religious susceptibilities. His was the task of convincing, without scandalizing, of correcting false notions as much by exploiting what was true and useful in them, as by exposing their essential fallacy.

The greatness of Hebrews lies in the success with which this task was accomplished. Even when the writer was intent on demonstrating the falsity of those notions, he was a master of tact. In seeking to persuade his readers to adopt a course of action which was repugnant to them, he took care to use their esteem for the Law, and also for their ancient Scriptures as a whole, as his starting point. Never did he belittle their existing heritage, but rather the reverse; yet never, in the process, did he fail to excite their preference for the new.

Thus he carefully stressed the glory of Moses; yet thereby he proved all the more convincingly the superior glory of Christ (3:1-6). He treated the Aaronic priesthood in the same way: its greatness for the readers lay in the divine appointment of Aaron to his office, but in emphasizing the importance of that fact he contrived to enhance the greatness of the appointment to which Christ himself was subject (5:1-5). In brief, he set out to show that, justified though they were in regarding what was theirs as being great, what they were thinking of discarding was immeasurably greater. He came to tell them of "a better hope" (7:19), of "better sacrifices" (9:23), of "a better covenant established upon better promises" (8:6) and of "a better and more perfect tabernacle" (9:11).[1]

## Christ in the Old Testament

In general, however, he employed a method of argument more convincing and effective still than that of directly confronting the Old with the New with a view to proving its inferiority. This was a novel method of comparison: to allay the misgivings of his readers at having to adhere to the New at the *expense* of the Old, he made a point of stressing the fundamental harmony between the two. This he did by interpreting the Old Testament *Christologically*. That is, all that Jesus was, and did, was convincingly shown to be only what Scripture had revealed symbolically to be essential to man's salvation (without itself being able to bring the same to realization). He used this method to prove that the Law, to which they wished to cling as an end in itself, was no more than a means – a divine means, true enough, but still only a means – to a yet greater end, the real and effectual reconciling of man to God. On this account, Hebrews is not so much an exposition of the Law and the Old Testament as a complete re-reading of them in the light of the new dispensation.

---

1. The point scarcely needs making that had not the readers all been Jews, and zealots for the Law, there would have been no point in this repeated argument *a fortiori*.

It assumes them to have been equally as Christian as that dispensation itself – with this sole (but, of course, essential) difference, that they spoke only in type and symbol. On that basis they are considered to acquire their real meaning, and to disclose their true message, only when reviewed in terms of Jesus, the Son of God and the Saviour of men.

The writer's application of this thesis had certain striking results. We find, for example, that not a single word of Jesus, as recorded in the Gospels, is quoted. Yet Jesus is made to speak in the epistle nonetheless! Statements are quoted as his which were, in the first instance, made by Old Testament writers or speakers. Thus to prove that Jesus, having died for sinners, was "not ashamed to call them brethren", the writer cites him as actually *saying*:

"I will declare thy name unto my brethren, in the midst of the church will I sing praise unto thee."

And, as though that were not enough, to this passage two further quotations are added:

"And again, I will put my trust in him. And again, Behold I and the children which God hath given me."
(Hebrews 2:11-13)

That is, without so much as giving a reason for so doing, the author calmly identifies the speaker in Psalm 22 as Jesus, and treats Isaiah – confessing his dependence upon God, and declaring himself and his children to be for signs and wonders in Israel – as a prefigurement of Christ in his humanity and in his oneness with those whom he came to save (cf. Psalm 22:22; Isaiah 8:17,18). The same procedure is adopted in the discussion later of the role of sacrifice. Jesus is quoted as having actually uttered words which are in fact found recorded in Psalm 40:6-8:

"When he cometh into the world, *he saith*, Sacrifice and offering thou wouldest not ... Then said I, Lo, I come ... to do thy will, O God."    (Hebrews 10:5-7)

It is the Psalmist who writes, but for the sender of the letter it is actually Jesus who speaks. Once again he does not explain, or excuse his method – he simply reads and interprets the Scriptures in terms of the Christ, and assumes that his readers are able both to follow his reasoning and to lend their assent to it.

**Crucifixion, Resurrection and Ascension**

We need scarcely remind ourselves why. They were Jews, and, as such, familiar with this procedure, dignified by rabbinical usage, of construing Scripture Messianically, and he in adopting it was using the method best calculated to gain their sympathetic hearing of his case. For that same reason he made only the scantiest reference to the biographical data to be found in the Gospels, though he and they were manifestly familiar with at least one of those records (e.g., 5:7; 7:14). He preferred, instead, as it were, to roll historical facts, and his comment on their significance, into one, and to express both simultaneously in language rich in Old Testament allusion and therefore of the greatest pertinence to his readers. Thus, instead of referring directly to the Crucifixion, he spoke of Jesus as "purging" our sins (1:3), or "sanctifying" the people by suffering "without the gate" (13:12). Likewise, instead of mentioning the Resurrection directly, he talked of Jesus being "saved from death" (5:7), or "brought again from the dead", through the blood of the everlasting covenant (13:20). The Ascension, too, is everywhere assumed in the letter, yet nowhere do we find it alluded to, except periphrastically as a "sitting down" by Jesus on the right hand of God (1:3), or the attainment by him of perfection (7:28), or his appearance on man's behalf in the very "presence of God" "beyond the veil" (9:24; 6:20). And the reason for this is obvious: in pursuance of his overriding aim, the author was demonstrating to his readers – and that with the assistance of the Law – that the Law was fulfilled by and in Jesus, being in fact, as later he boldly states, only "a *shadow* of good things to come", and not "the very image" of those things (10:1).

Though less obvious – and, for that reason, easily missed – a secondary intention can, however, also be detected in these passages – that of confirming the readers' faith in the Resurrection and Ascension as such. For is it conceivable that those Christians – even though Jews – should think of forsaking Christ while their faith in the Resurrection and Ascension was still *robust*? What can a writer, so skilled in argument as ours, be doing, by insisting on the "*immutability*" of God's counsel, other than calming doubts in his readers' minds about these very matters? (6:17). Why assure them, again, that they have need of patience, "for yet a little while, and he that shall come *will* come", unless they are in peril of "casting away" their confidence in the coming of Christ (10:35-37)?

Regarding the Crucifixion – as a fact in itself – there was, of course, no doubt. What had become so debatable for them was its *significance*, and it was on that account that the writer had so strenuously to insist, as we shall see, on its propriety and necessity. But if they – and there was a distinct danger of this – adopted the judgement passed by their unbelieving brethren upon the fact that Jesus was crucified, then clearly their faith in his Resurrection and Ascension – and therefore in his intercessory activity on their behalf – could not possibly survive. They would be compelled, after all, to write off him whom once they had confessed as Lord, as an imposter, and his death as devoid of saving power. And the converse would also be true: were there the slightest faltering in their conviction that the Resurrection and Ascension were authentic facts, their faith in its saving power would sooner or later assuredly perish.

### Dealing with three attitudes

These considerations enable us to review the writer's arguments in a fresh light: time and again it will help us, in the attempt to follow his thought – especially at its most intricate – to bear in mind how many were the factors of which he had to take account when writing. He was aware of much concerning his readers about which we are not informed (except in the measure that we can infer it by scrutinizing his comments with special care). To not only one, but to a whole host of needs, would his epistle have to be adjusted. He would need to deal, here with the anguish of the convinced but timid; there with the genuine doubts of the waverers and the disillusioned; elsewhere with the sophistry – and even the hostility – of those who were concerned only with the safety of their skin. There can be no doubt, in fact, that where he is (for us, that is) at his obscurest, he is writing with an eye to all these three things at once, and this for one obvious reason – occasionally, the anguish, the doubts and the sophistry in question would all be related to *one and the same topic*.

We have an excellent illustration of this in the long homiletic digression extending from 3:6 to 4:11. Looked at cursorily, the first and last verses of this section would seem to have no connection whatever. One talks of Christians constituting Christ's "house"; the other of their entering into God's rest. Both, however, have to do with *persistence* – the one with persistence in faith, the other with persistence in effort – and that common theme forms the link between them, as between all the seemingly tortuous argument which extends from one to the other. Let us now tenaciously follow the course of the writer's thought to see how true this is.

**Chapter 3 verses 6-11**

To prove that we Christians form God's "house" provided we hold fast the confidence and the rejoicing of the hope firm *unto the end*, the author quotes the following verses from Psalm 95 as the Spirit's message to them:

"Today if ye will hear his voice, harden not your hearts, as in the provocation, in the day of temptation in the wilderness: when your fathers tempted me, proved me, and saw my works forty years. Wherefore I was grieved with that generation, and said, They do alway err in their heart; and they have not known my ways. So I sware in my wrath, They shall not enter into my rest." (verses 7-11)

## Verse 12

Resuming his argument on the need for persistence, the author begins to expound the significance of the psalm in terms of his readers' circumstances, quoting phrase after phrase as warnings to them. Here the play is on the word "*heart*". To counter their intention of letting go their faith, and to drive home his exhortation to them to "hold fast", he warns them specifically against "an *evil* heart" – which he styles also, "a heart of *unbelief*" – lest they depart from the living God. The term "unbelief" is allusive – doubly so: it diagnoses the reason for the failure and punishment of their forefathers; and it also rebukes the readers themselves for their own loss of faith. For they too, in their turn, have witnessed God's works – and that for forty years(?)[2] – God having borne witness to the truth of the word preached to them, "both with signs and wonders, and with divers miracles, and gifts of the Holy Spirit, according to his own will" (2:4).

## Verse 13

The words, "Today" and "harden", now bear the stress and come in for adaptation to their own case. It is "the living God" with whom they have to do, as did their fathers, and they are bidden to seize their opportunity while it still lasts – while the term, "Today" still remains valid. "Exhort one another daily, while it is called Today", says he, "lest any of you be *hardened* through the deceitfulness of sin". Here, manifestly, he is putting them on their guard against subtle propaganda which threatens to subvert them. If they fall victim to it they will thereby become "hardened" against "hearing the voice" of God Himself addressing them through the Psalmist (cf. 12:25, and also 1:1,2).

---

2. In the quotation of the psalm the author transposes the term "forty years", and applies it to the period during which their fathers saw God's works, instead of to the period during which they provoked God. Is he making the parallel with their own experience all the more pointed because a period of that duration had elapsed? It might well be, since this would bring us to the very eve of the fall of Jerusalem. At all events, in 3:17 he replaces the term in its correct position.

He at once proceeds to warn them what disaster will in that event ensue – exploiting to the full the moral drawn by the Psalmist from the fate of the faithless in the wilderness (Numbers 14:22,23,28-30).

## Verse 14

First he restates his introductory proposition – the theme (for such it is) of the entire argument:

> "For we are made partakers of Christ, if we hold the beginning of our confidence stedfast *unto the end.*"

## Verse 15

He now quotes a verse of the psalm in his support – a verse which pithily cautions them against the fault of their fathers in failing to retain the confidence which brought them out of Egypt "stedfast unto the end".

> "Today if ye will hear his voice, harden not your hearts, as in the provocation."

*God* is appealing to them – let them therefore not offer resistance to His approach!

## Verses 16-19

"Provocation" now becomes the keyword. Tactfully he reminds them that the evil disposition of heart in their fathers "provoked" God, and moved Him to punitive action – and that, be it noted, against the very people whom He had done so much to deliver from Egypt![3] So doing he warns them of the peril in which they are placing themselves. The sentence of God expressly excluded the rebels from the enjoyment of His Rest. To such a pass did their lack of faith in God bring them. "So we see", he concludes, "that they could not enter in *because of unbelief*", thus driving home his warning against "an evil heart of unbelief" in the readers.

---

3. Here, once again, we encounter one of those subtle shafts against the trust being placed by the readers, as Jews, in their racial privileges. That they belonged to the people whom God had declared to be His by bringing them out of Egypt, did not exempt them from sharing the fate of the rebellious among that people. *Flesh descent was valueless in itself.*

After warning comes encouragement. God, in excluding some on account of their unbelief, at the same time reaffirmed the right of others – that is, those with faith, to enter His Rest. Contrast, "Surely they *shall not see* the land" (Numbers 14:23), with "But my servant Caleb, because he had another spirit with him ... him will I *bring into* the land" (verse 24).

## Chapter 4 verses 1,2

"Rest" has in the preceding verses become the keyword, and remains so now till the end of the argument. In this transition the implications of 3:17-19 are made explicit for the writer's Christian readers. They too, receiving a promise of Rest, can if unbelieving be excluded from it; or, if believing, can be admitted to it – the psalm being witness.

Here the argument becomes especially hard to follow, but the conclusion drawn towards its end – "There remaineth therefore a rest to the people of God" (4:9) – reveals that the writer is having to *vindicate* the notion that the Rest which God ultimately envisaged for man is still future and not yet realized. Seeing it is to Jews that he writes, he must therefore be countering a belief that the Rest had been initiated by the settlement in the Land under Joshua and so was not meant to constitute more than that.[4]

## Verses 3-7

Boldly he construes the sentence of exclusion as proof that "We which have believed *do* enter". But so doing he is arguing in terms of his own assertion, and has to deal now with the scepticism which challenges that assertion. This he does, first by pointing out that this sentence – pronounced in Moses' day – spoke of God's Rest long after the cessation of His creative work on the seventh day. But it evidently envisaged the same Rest

---

4. This gives us some insight into what the writer meant by "an evil heart of unbelief". It is rank materialism it seems, that he is here countering – a denial of the very notion of a life to come. Might not this be also why he insists so often in the letter that the Christian's reward is one "to come" and to be patiently awaited?

– and not some other about to be enjoyed in Canaan – because the very terms used in the wilderness *before* the entry into the land were used again by the Psalmist, long *after* that entry, with the intimation – implicit in the pointed use of the word, "Today" that the invitation to men to enjoy this Rest was still binding, God being again the speaker on the principle of 1:1.

"Again *he* limiteth a certain day, *saying in David*, Today, *after so long a time*; as it is said, Today if ye will hear his voice, harden not your hearts."

**Verses 8-10**

The writer can now expose the falsity of the view that the Rest promised was simply the rest achieved through the conquest of Joshua. To speak *afterward* of another day was proof in itself that the Rest in question was not already achieved, but one still future even to David's day. And the "Today" not yet having expired, the Rest was still future also to the readers' day: "There *remaineth* therefore a rest to the people of God."

But so long as the Rest tarries the lot of man is to work. Not until His work had ceased did God rest. The same is true for man. The time of waiting is a time of *effort* and this must not cease until the Day of Rest dawns.

**Verse 11**

So, skilfully the argument is brought round to the point of departure. Despite all the incidental refutations of false teaching which he has had to make, the author has not forgotten his original intention. Changing now his metaphor, and couching his exhortation in terms of the psalm which he has quoted against the dispirited and the obstinate, he stresses anew the need to put effort out *to the very end*:

"Let us *labour* therefore to enter into that rest [says he] lest any man fall after the example of unbelief."

Thus does the author contrive to handle several themes at once. His habit of doing so makes his reasoning hard for us to follow in such passages. But there would be no obscurity for his readers: they would feel the full weight of his blows, and we need to remind ourselves constantly of that fact. We must always be at pains to perceive, by inference, the polemical purpose of each observation which he made, for so doing we enter, as it were, into his readers' situation, and begin to understand the epistle as they themselves understood it. That is our fundamental task throughout, and this means of assimilating the idiom of thought in the epistle is an essential part of it.

## A future Day of Rest

We note that everything depended for the author (when confronted by the assertion of some that the Rest had already begun) upon the fact that the Psalmist had renewed God's invitation to enter that Rest, "*after so long a time*" (4:7).

"If [Joshua] had given them rest [he argued] then would he not *afterward* have spoken of another day." (verse 8)

It is interesting to observe the same deductive reasoning being employed by him in other contexts also. Standing by the Law, his readers, naturally, stood closely by the established priesthood as well. For them the appointment of the Aaronic family to priestly office was of permanent validity. The writer's rejoinder was masterly: long *after* Aaron's time, promise had been made on oath to the Messiah (for who but the Messiah could he be who was exalted to the right hand of God?), that he should be priest for ever after the order of Melchizedek (Psalm 110:4).

"If therefore [reasoned the author] perfection were by the Levitical priesthood ... what *further* need was there that *another* priest should rise after the order of *Melchisedec*, and not be called after the order of *Aaron*?" (7:11)

The "word of the oath", as he called it, was "*since* the law" – that is, *subsequent* to it – so there could be no doubt of the intention with which it was spoken (verse 28). And the same, he insisted, was true of Jeremiah's announcement of the making of a New Covenant. It was "new" because coming later than that made at Sinai:

"In that he saith, A new covenant, he hath made the first old." (8:13)

**Covenant or testament?**

In this latter passage, about the sense of the word *diatheke*, to be found in the original Greek text of Hebrews, there can be no doubt at all. It signified "covenant" and is rightly so rendered here. The same word, however, occurs sixteen more times in Hebrews. On ten of these occasions, consistently with this passage, it is again rendered "covenant". The problem is to know why it is rendered on the six remaining occasions by the alternative word "testament". In 7:22 the rendering, "testament" is manifestly indefensible – Jesus is the surety of a *covenant*, not of a testament. The same is true of the renderings, "the new testament", "the first testament" in 9:15, and, "the testament which God hath enjoined", in 9:20. No linguistic proof need be advanced to prove that in calling Jesus the "mediator of the new *diatheke*" the author was contrasting him pointedly with Moses, the mediator of the old, and that he again had Jeremiah's words in mind: "testament" here ought clearly to have been "covenant". So, again, immediately afterwards – Jesus died "for the redemption of transgressions" committed under the first *covenant*, not testament. As for 9:20, as this is a quotation of Moses' own words concerning "the blood of the covenant" (Exodus 24:8), one marvels that the translators should even have entertained the idea of rendering *diatheke* by "testament": in doing so they were clearly at fault. What, then, of the remaining two cases? Do we accept or reject "testament" there? Scholars are divided. That *diatheke* strongly suggested a legal disposition of property and estate – our modern "will" – is indisputable. In secular writings it had in fact no other connotation. This prompts the question as to why it was used by the author to render the word "covenant". The answer is simple. The translators of the Septuagint version had appropriated the term and attached this special Hebrew sense to it. It thus lay ready to hand for the author's use, and had moreover, the weight of authority and tradition behind it for his readers – they being *Jews*. The problem, then, is to decide in what sense he intended to use the term in 9:16,17, which in the A.V. read thus:

"For where a testament is, there must also of necessity be the death of the testator. For a testament is of force after men are dead: otherwise it is of no strength at all while the testator liveth."

Why the A.V. translators and others should render *diatheke* here by "testament" is obvious: these axioms, viewed in isolation, apply perfectly in the case of a testament (i.e., a will). They should, however, not be so viewed exclusively. For they are set in a context – first, the immediate context, one where, despite the translators' choice, "covenant" has to be preferred to "testament", and one to which the conjunction "for" closely relates them in strict sequence of thought; secondly, the general context of the epistle, whose atmosphere and terminology are wholly Jewish, in accordance with the circumstances which called it forth. Is it conceivable that to convince Jews – zealous of the Law – of the truth of his contentions, the author should advert to a purely *Gentile* practice? Manifestly, no. Despite all linguistic evidence to be quoted in favour of "testament", the insertion of the term here is an anachronism, destructive of the sequence of the thought in a passage where the sequence of the thought is of paramount importance. True, the writer's meaning is not immediately clear even when "covenant" is substituted in the place of "testament". But, once again, that is because terms, rich in allusiveness for the first readers, lack that allusiveness for us. This handicap we can overcome only by careful reference to the Old Testament.

What do we there find? That all covenants between God and man were ratified by *blood* (i.e., death): even the first covenant between God and Israel, as the writer here argues, "was dedicated with blood" (9:18). The same, earlier still, was also true of God's covenant with Abraham: it was over the dead bodies of animals and birds that the covenant was made (Genesis 15:8-18). The lesson taught was that man, being a sinner, needed to be reconciled to God by sacrifice, before God could with propriety enter into solemn agreement with him – i.e., that "without shedding of blood there is no remission" whatsoever (Hebrews 9:22). The human partner in the covenant always gave his assent to this profound truth by seeing himself symbolized in the animals sacrificed, and by regarding their death as tantamount to his own. The wonder of the New Covenant, as we shall see better later, was that Christ was at once the mediator, *and* the sacrifice, and upheld in his *own* death the unalterable truth that "where a testament (i.e., a covenant) is, there must also of necessity be the death of the testator (i.e., covenant maker – on the *human* side)". It was a singular coincidence[5] that here, in terms of words only, the axiom was equally as valid for a disposition of personal property before death, according to Greek custom, as for solemn covenant between God and man, according to Jewish custom. The fact remained, however, that, in stating that "a testament is of force where there hath been death" (9:17, R.V.), the author envisaged only Old Testament practice, since this alone, let it always be remembered, would have authority for his readers. For never must we escape from the atmosphere of the epistle if we wish to understand it aright. The fact is that Hebrews was a letter written by a Jew, for the express benefit of Jews, and that about matters of direct and passionate concern to none but Jews. To construe it otherwise is to stultify the attempt to understand it aright. In this passage for all its ambiguity for us, the author was, as everywhere else, seeking to persuade his readers – for whom that ambiguity did not exist –

---

5. There is no reason to suppose, of course, that this coincidence had not struck the author himself.

that the Law was no longer binding and should now be abandoned, the New Covenant having replaced the Old.

## Things that cannot be shaken

He knew, as we have seen, that any conviction to the contrary was in any case soon to be rudely disillusioned. The polity which his readers were being urged to uphold was shortly to be brought to ruin. The days of Jerusalem, of the Temple, and thus of the operation of the Law, were numbered. He, being one of themselves, knew what an overpowering shock it would be for them to find out for the first time, in the face of the tragedy itself, that what they fondly thought to be stable had proved to be the very opposite. He felt in himself – what we can only divine second-hand – the utter despair which would take possession of them as the very bottom fell out of their world. Hence his strenuous insistence that there *are* things that abide and that cannot be shaken (12:27); that Christians possess "a kingdom which cannot be moved" (verse 28); that the end of their conversation is one who is "the same yesterday, and today, and for ever" (13:7,8). Everywhere, in fact, we find him preoccupied with the contrast between the temporal and the timeless. The note is struck early in the epistle: the transience of created things is contrasted with the permanence of Him who caused them to be brought into being:

"They shall perish; but thou remainest; and they all shall wax old ... and they shall be changed: but thou art the same, and thy years shall not fail."

(1:11,12)

The same note is struck afresh thereafter in a wide variety of contexts: Moses fades before Christ; the Aaronic priesthood before that of Melchizedek; the material Tabernacle before the true; the "same sacrifices", offered "oftentimes", before the one offering of permanent efficacy; the "pleasures of sin for a season", before the recompense of the reward"; and, of course, the earthly heritage before the "heavenly" – be it a case of the Holy Land, or of the Holy City.

These faltering Christians should see their calling as a *heavenly* one (3:1), and themselves therefore as related only to "heavenly things" (9:23) – and related to them moreover, *here and now*.

## Experiencing the future in the present

For if the gaze of Christians is essentially to be turned towards "things to come", that does not alter the fact that they should endure as already "seeing him who is invisible" (11:27); regard their hope as one which already "entereth into that within the veil" (6:19); recognize the possession of the Spirit as a tasting in advance of the powers of the world to come (verse 5); console themselves, when bereft of worldly possessions, with the knowledge that they "have in *heaven* a better and an enduring substance" (10:36). This they can do only through the exercise of faith, for "faith is the substance of things hoped for, the evidence of things not seen" – proof in itself of the reality of those things, the instrument whereby the barriers of space and time can be surmounted even now (11:1). It gives man immediate experience of the spiritual reality which lies beyond this palpable world (verse 3).

It is that reality which is of transcendent importance for the author, and towards which he seeks to divert the gaze of his readers from those tangible things – a material sanctuary, a ceremonial worship, mere animal sacrifices – with which they are engrossed. Amid a shaking world he comes to them with the assurance of the endurance and solidity of their Christian hope. It is an *anchor* of the soul, something *sure* and *steadfast* (6:19), a *strong* consolation (verse 18). Christ can save to the *uttermost* (7:25). The apostles' witness has been directly *confirmed* by God (2:3), and God's own promise has been attested by an *oath* (6:16,17). Jesus is therefore a *surety* of a better covenant (7:22). All that is needed is for them to *hold fast* (10:23), to be *established* (13:9), to *endure* like Moses (11:27) and all the other Old Testament heroes whom he has brought to their notice (verses 32-40).

## Intellectual difficulties addressed

The author realizes that, for some of his readers at least, the difficulties seem insurmountable. For certain of them, those difficulties are primarily intellectual. The fact that Jesus died seems proof to them that his claims to be the Christ were false. This suggestion the writer refutes by demonstrating the suffering and humiliation of the Saviour to be the secret of his glorification (2:9,10). For others the long delay in receiving the promise, and the non-appearance of Jesus to them in their trial, have bred doubt and a feeling that the Lord no longer interests himself in their case. To them the author replies by showing the absence of Jesus to be rather an appearance on their behalf in heaven (9:24), and an opening up for them of the way to God (10:19,20). For others, again, the difficulties are more of a practical order: they fear to remain loyal to Christ because they fear death more. By way of reply the writer reminds them that even Jesus himself shrank from death – yet that despite this, he was obedient to the call to undergo it, and was saved on that account (5:7,8). Jesus, declares the writer, having himself suffered and himself been saved can, and does, feel for them in their present ordeal, and will just as assuredly save them, if they in their turn are obedient to him as he was to God (4:15; 5:9).

Even of the moral decline of a certain section of his readers the author finds time to take account. In seeking to "lift up the hands which hang down, and the feeble knees", he does not neglect to enjoin holiness and purity of life as well as courage and fortitude (12:12-17). When read only cursorily, the closing chapter of the epistle might appear a rather lame appendage to the discussion of the grand central themes which go before it, but it is obvious upon reflection that here, once more, his remarks would for some of his readers have an especial pertinence. Some were guilty of sowing discord and strife; of refusing hospitality to the needy and fugitive; of neglecting those of their brethren who had already been imprisoned, in case they should share their fate; of abandoning moral restraint as well as their hope, and of setting their minds wholly on material things (13:1-5). The writer reminds them of their duty, reminds them too that they are accountable to God – God whom he has just defined as a consuming fire (12:29).

Thus where one group, or another, among his readers stood in need of help, or of reassurance, or of reprimand, there stood the writer ready to act, bidding them "hold fast ... firm unto the end" (3:6). Never was a community better served in the hour of peril. Sorry indeed must have been the state of heart and mind of any who spurned his help. They were indeed wanton traitors to their holy calling.

# 3

## "HE SHALL BE TO ME A SON"
*The finality of the new revelation.*

TO divorce Hebrews from the situation to which it was a premeditated answer is to ruin all hope of understanding it aright. Already it has become abundantly evident that had there not been a certain group of Jewish Christians who, in the face both of Scripture prophecy and of the portentous trend of contemporary events, persisted in believing the Law to be immutable and adherence to it to be a matter of solemn religious duty, the epistle would never have seen the light.

From the very outset the writer is making assault upon a fixed position in which his readers are entrenched, and from which, with every weapon in his armoury, he seeks to dislodge them. Not an argument is used except with that one object in mind, so that we cannot too often remind ourselves that wherever his reasoning is for us more than usually difficult to follow, it must, if we are to make proper sense of it, be construed in the light of the peculiar situation which called it forth.

True in all cases, this is especially true of the first chapter of the epistle and of other passages in kindred vein.

**Correcting false beliefs**
Nowhere is the writer more palpably seeking to put wrong notions right than there. A note almost of disdain – certainly of exasperation – comes sounding through his rhetorical questions.

"For unto which of the *angels* [he asks, confident that no answer will – or can – be given] said he at any time, Thou art my Son, this day have I begotten thee?" (1:5)

And the same, yet again:

"But to which of the *angels* said he at any time, Sit on my right hand, until I make thine enemies thy footstool?" (verse 13)

There would, manifestly, have been no sense in such questions, had they not exposed some folly on the part of the readers, and this consideration obliges us at once to enquire the explanation for their – and so for his – concern with this particular topic of angels. We have not far to seek. His first bolts discharged, and so their first defences breached, he forthwith sounds the solemn warning:

"Therefore we ought to give the more earnest heed to the things which we have heard, lest at any time we should let them slip." (2:1)

## A higher authority

"More earnest": the words were pregnant with meaning, implying especially that there was need of a progression forward from an established earnestness, already considerable, to an earnestness greater yet. But why this established earnestness, in the first place? Because, says the writer, "the word spoken by *angels*" was "stedfast", the proof being that "every transgression and disobedience" committed against it "received a just recompence of reward" (verse 2), Here, then, lies the secret of his concern with angels: their status was for him – and so for his readers (otherwise he reasoned against them in vain) – the measure of the authority of some "word" which had been "spoken" by them. It was because their status was so elevated that the sanctions attaching to that "word" were so severe; no flouting of their authority could escape unpunished. But how came the need, in view of this, for an earnestness even greater still on the part of those who had of late heard some other "word"? Manifestly, one thing only could explain it: this new word – "the things which we have heard" – had been "spoken" by one who was of a rank

– and so, once again, of an authority – higher far than that of angels. That is, the essential issue throughout this discussion is not that of rank as such, but of the authority attaching to it. Never must that fact be lost from sight.

## A change of preference

Noticeable at once in this warning, as so often elsewhere in the epistle, is the author's resort to periphrastic expressions. These inevitably puzzle us: but for these first readers they were clearly assumed to interpret themselves. Happily even for us, with so suggestive a context to help us, they present no difficulty here. The expressions, "the things which we have heard" (2:1), and the "great salvation which at the first began to be spoken by the Lord" (verse 3), were manifestly meant to signify that Christian preaching which these Jewish readers had once been so eager to hear and to believe. Conversely, in the circumstances, what else could have been meant by "the word spoken by angels" (with which that preaching is at once compared and contrasted with such skill and tact), other than the Law given to their fathers at Sinai "by the disposition of angels"? (Acts 7:53). As we have already so often had occasion to note, the consistent contrast in this letter is *between the Law and the Gospel*. Hitherto the readers have had both. The time has now come when they must relinquish either the one or the other. Their natural preference is for the Law. But the purpose of the epistle is to change this into a preference for the Gospel, and the argumentation of the opening chapter is but the first stage in the implementation of that purpose – as the warning predicated upon it immediately afterwards goes so convincingly to show. So, to be understood by us, as it was understood – and meant to be understood – by the original readers, it must clearly be read in the light of that overriding fact.

## The status of the angels

So read what does it tell us? This much at once, on the score of the emphatic contrast drawn between

Christ and the angels – that the readers were strongly inclined to ascribe to these an authority higher than that of their Lord! That they should ever entertain such a notion may indeed appal and mystify us; yet not otherwise would the sender have chosen to contend against them in the form in which he did in this section. It was clearly the form assumed by their arguments which decided the form of his own in reply. Besides, we know, because he himself revealed the fact, that they were an easy prey to certain "divers and strange doctrines", as he called them (13:9). On that score what more probable than that some at least of those doctrines were being directly refuted in the letter? This was indeed one of the strangest of them all. But the extravagance of the notion shows to what desperate lengths the readers were being driven in their attempt to vindicate a continued loyalty to the Law *if necessary at the cost of renouncing Christ*!

Returning now to the arguments marshalled in this chapter, we find the author poised, in 1:4, to take his readers' absurd position by storm. He was well placed to do this – and that thanks even more to his own skill than to their folly. For he had fully prepared himself for the assault. Knowing only too well that unless his case had the whole weight of Old Testament Scripture behind it the failure of his appeal to them was a foregone conclusion, he had resolved to open his epistle with an emphatic assertion of the authority of that Scripture as the authentic Word of God. But he had resolved too, that there should be an equally emphatic assertion of yet another supremely important truth, which if it was one his readers did not as yet openly disavow, was one which they were nevertheless coming perilously close to challenging. This was that God, besides speaking of yore in the prophets to their ancestors, had again, in their very own day, spoken anew in Christ whom they were being pressed, by their unbelieving brethren, to forsake. Yet the prime need of the readers was not so much to have this truth reaffirmed, as to have its implications made plain to them.

## The exaltation of Christ

But how? In one way only: if the process was to serve any useful purpose those implications had of necessity to be expressed in terms of their present situation. And what situation was that? The desperate situation of not knowing whether to rank Christ above Moses, i.e., the Gospel above the Law. So with a deft choice of phraseology, redolent of the Law and of the ancient Scriptures as a whole, the writer revealed to them the nature of God's speaking in Christ:

"God, who at sundry times and in divers manners spake in time past unto the fathers by the prophets, hath in these last days spoken unto us by his Son, whom he hath appointed heir of all things, by whom also he made the worlds; who being the brightness of his glory, and the express image of his person, and upholding all things by the word of his power, when he had by himself purged our sins, sat down on the right hand of the Majesty on high; being made so much better than the angels, as he hath by inheritance obtained a more excellent name than they." (1:1-4)

Taking the last assertion as our starting point, since its connection with the following argument is so intimate, we find the writer resorting at once to Scripture in support of its truth. This he was all the more forcefully able to do through having so categorically affirmed the authority of the Old Testament at the very outset. The readers in leaning to the view that Jesus was inferior to angels, probably pleaded in support of it the fact that he had been a mere man – that is, had been made *lower* than the angels. With this particular matter the author would in due course deal at length. But his immediate concern here was to bring his readers face to face with *present* reality – which was that Jesus had by now been made unquestionably *better* than the angels, a fact established by the superior name conferred upon him. For the present, then, the writer had eyes only for the *exalted* Jesus. Reading first Psalm

## "HE SHALL BE TO ME A SON"

2, and then the covenant made with David (2 Samuel 7:14), Christologically, he saw Jesus, even before his first appearing, acknowledged prophetically by God as *Son*. The readers, being fully familiar with the Hebrew idiom of the passages here cited, would perceive at once the stress there laid on the concept of Sonship. But compelled to acknowledge in Jesus the Son of God, were they thereby compelled also to see in him one superior to angels? The proof here advanced was only an argument from silence so far as that matter was concerned, and thus for them was not of necessity conclusive. But, to settle all doubt, an explicit Scripture swiftly followed – one stressing the elevation over angels which awaits the Son, as *Firstborn*, at his Second Advent:

"When he again bringeth in the firstborn into the world, he saith, And let all the angels of God worship him." (1:6, RV)

Here, then, was proof positive: far from Jesus being of lesser rank than the angels, they for their part were destined to be subordinated to him, and were now called upon by God Himself to acknowledge his supremacy. Not theirs to rule, but his alone.

"Of the angels he saith, Who maketh his angels spirits, and his ministers a flame of fire. But of the Son he saith, Thy throne, O God, is for ever and ever; a sceptre of righteousness is the sceptre of thy kingdom." (verses 7,8)

To them is attributed in the changed situation the title, "Ministers" alone; but to him, that of "God". Such is the measure of his exaltation. His probation lies behind him now as he sits enthroned beside God, and by God – "Thou has loved righteousness, and hated iniquity; *therefore* God, even thy God, hath anointed thee with the oil of gladness above thy fellows" (verse 9). Could there possibly be clearer evidence than that, either advanced or needed, that he had become "so much *better* than the angels"?

## The Law superseded

And there the author would have been fully warranted in terminating his argument. But only if his concern had been simply to prove the Gospel to be superior to the Law. This, however, was only half his purpose; there remained another and far more difficult task – that of convincing his readers that, precisely because the Gospel was above the Law, it had in addition rendered it obsolete. For looking afresh at the warning given in 2:1-4 we now find that not only the first fact, but also the second, was by the writer now regarded as sufficiently evident for his warning to be predicated on both alike. He spoke significantly of the Law as something which *"was* stedfast": *"was"* – obviously because it had ceased to be so at the time of writing.

But it is obvious that by this stage his readers would not for one moment have construed the superiority of the Gospel to the Law to mean the *replacement* of the latter by the former unless they had actually been compelled by the writer to do so. That is, he could not have thus calmly presupposed the passing of the Law, when framing this first solemn warning, unless he had already sought to demonstrate that passing to be a fact, and felt confident that he had demonstrated it convincingly.

Now up to 1:9, the writer was still clearly preoccupied with questions of status. At what stage then did he turn to the burning issue, which is of such capital interest in the epistle as a whole, and which was indeed its very *raison d'être* – that of the need actually to *discard* the Law? Clearly it was somewhere between that point and the warning in which the obsolescence of the Law was taken so naturally for granted – that is, in the remainder of the first chapter. Let the quotation of Psalm 102:25-27 now be read with this factor, and with the whole aim of the epistle, carefully kept in mind, and its phraseology at once becomes positively luminous:

"And, Thou, Lord, in the beginning hast laid the foundation of the earth; and the heavens are the

works of thine hands: they shall perish; but thou remainest; and they all shall wax old as doth a garment; and as a vesture shalt thou fold them up, and they shall be changed: but thou art the same, and thy years shall not fail." (Hebrews 1:10-12)
Here, manifestly, is the changing of an established order, and the survival and endurance of another. And, to clinch it as proof of the superiority of the work and mission of the Son over that of the angels, the writer adds to it also the weighty rhetorical question:

"But to which of the angels said he at any time, Sit on my right hand, until I make thine enemies thy footstool?" (verse 13)

The angels, he concluded, were mere "ministering spirits" – lacking in powers of initiative and independent action, "sent forth to minister for them who shall be heirs of salvation" (verse 14). There was not the permanence in their work that there was in the Son's.

So that was the reason, then, why it should be at this particular point that he chose to sound his warning. Faced with the need to discard either the Gospel or the Law, his readers were disposed to discard the Gospel. But this was to give the lesser preference over the greater! This should now be plain to them, so that henceforth there was no excuse for their folly. Thus before continuing his argument, and proceeding to reconcile the initial humiliation of the Son with his ultimate glorification (2:5-18), the writer would spare the time to point this out to them in the very plainest terms (verses 1-4).

### Heavens and earth to perish

So now let us see the precise bearing of the quotation of Psalm 102 on the argument, not only here, but also elsewhere in the letter. On the one hand we find ranged an "earth" and "heavens" which are destined to "perish", "wax old", be "folded up" and "be changed": on the other hand there stands the "Lord" who made them, whose destiny, in contrast is to "remain" and be "the same". The author's intention was clearly that these mutable things should be taken to signify the Law, whereas the one who continues beyond it, and sees it pass away, is the "Lord" who spoke that "great salvation" of which the authority was so much higher than "the word spoken by angels", and who is "the same yesterday, today and for ever" (13:8).

The rest of the epistle triumphantly vindicates this conclusion. The crowning argument of chapter 12 is that in the coming convulsion – which will sweep away City, Temple, and Law together, in one definitive act of divine judgement, irrevocable in its consequences – the promise of God will be fulfilled:

"Yet once more I shake *not the earth only*, but also heaven." (12:26)

This cataclysm is construed by the writer as a *promise* because it is the pledge of the fact that Jesus is the mediator of the *New* Covenant (verse 24) – new, not only in the sense of 8:13, but also new in *kind*, distinct in its benefits – which has related the Christian to "a kingdom which cannot be moved". And before that stage, when actually contrasting the two Covenants, the author has applied to the passing of the old the very terminology of Psalm 102:26,27:

"Now that which decayeth and waxeth old is ready to vanish away."

And everywhere, of course, in the letter the generation in which the writer and readers live is regarded as a veritable end of the world: the Son has appeared "in these last days" (1:2), "once in the end of the world" (9:26). This is "the time of reformation" (verse 10). One has only to think of Peter's comments on the same topic (2 Peter 3:10-13), and to realize that they are themselves also an adaptation of prophetic language (Isaiah 65:17), to appreciate how apt, and how meaningful, this figurative language would be to the readers. The writer was conditioning their minds to accept the passing away of the old order to give place to the new.

## The Law a mere shadow

To our prosaic western minds the language used is disconcerting, but once again, the better we understand the idiom of thought in the epistle, the more plainly it speaks to us. For us there is no need to prove that it is not the angels but to the Son of Man that "the world to come" – that is, the abiding spiritual reality one day to be made manifest – has been made subject (2:5), but there was a distinct need of it for these first readers, since with that issue the problem of the continued validity of the Law was for them so intimately bound up. "Change" for them spelt a complete revolution in their thinking (1:12; 7:12). It was signal proof that the Law was after all not "heavenly", but earthly; that it was a mere "shadow of heavenly things" (8:5), insubstantial, preparatory not permanent (1:14). To convince them of just that fact was the aim of the writer in interpreting Psalm 102:25-27 Christologically, and in seeing in language applied originally to God, language which could with perfect propriety be applied also to the Son.

Wherein lay the propriety? Even granting that the language of the psalm can be adapted to the spiritual order established through Moses, in what sense could "the heavens" and "the earth" so founded be said to be the work of *Christ's* hands? Inasmuch as the Law was "the word spoken by angels", it would seem more appropriate rather to describe these as the work of *their* hands. But for the readers to have made this rejoinder would not have helped their cause one whit. Rather would it have emphasized the transience of the Law, and done that cause greater harm. And even if, instead, they insisted that Psalm 102 envisaged solely the natural creation they would have in no way invalidated the writer's case, for they would have merely enhanced thereby the stature of the Son and confirmed his superiority to the angels whom they believed (and rightly) to have been also the agents of creation. The best they could have done was challenge the author's right to interpret the psalm Christologically, for the polemical intention with which he quoted it would at once be obvious to them – as now it is to us.

## Interpreting Psalm 102 Christologically

What right, then, had he to do so? He had taken care to state it at the outset. There he had insisted that in the final analysis there is only one speaker – God Himself (as elsewhere he remained true to Old Testament teaching in insisting that God is likewise the ultimate Creator and Cause of all things: 2:10; 3:4; 11:3). But God has always spoken to men through the medium of men; the highest medium of all, however, was Christ – for he was more than man.

> "God [stated the author], who at sundry times and in divers manners spake in times past unto the fathers in the prophets, hath in these last days spoken unto us in a Son." (1:1,2)

"In a *Son*": here was revelation not only different in scope and content (thus making good the deficiencies of the Old Testament which though divine was incomplete), but different in *kind* from all that had gone before. Here was not a prophet only but a Son, a veritable embodiment in flesh of the divine utterance. In him God was vocal to the extent of being personally identifiable with him, as Father with Son – a truth which the writer expressed by declaring him to have been – and still to be (for time in no way alters this quality of being) – the effulgence, or bodying forth, of the Father's personal glory, as true a representation in flesh of what God is as is the impression left in wax or metal of the die which made it (verse 3).

In these profound words the readers, being Jews, would perceive an allusion to the moral glory of God and catch an insight into the meaning of His Name (Exodus 33:18,19; 34:5-7). They would see the author pointing to Jesus as the realization in a human life of the great concept symbolically expressed in the Tabernacle, the abode of God's glory. And in so doing they would perceive, too, a hint that behind the material things of their religion, with which they were so pathetically engrossed, lay a deeper reality which had of late been revealed to them in the Son – an eternal order to which he belonged by right of birth, and concerning which the epistle would have so much to tell them, both to loosen their hold on the Law and to tighten their hold on Christ (cf. pp. 26,27). As, then, the Son showed forth God to men, so conversely what was written of God was applicable to him in the measure that he was himself divine. His birth as Son – which was in time (1:2,5) – was foreordained before time. The speaking which began "in the beginning" when "God said", and "it was so" (Genesis 1:1-3), when He "spake" His Word and "it was done" (Psalm 33:6,9), culminated in him; and in and through him the original creative purpose with man will eventually be realized (2:6-10). As the writer to the Hebrews himself expressed it, it was through the Son that God "made the ages" (1:2), so that he in his own person bears them on to their appointed end – i.e., he "upholds all things by the Word of his (God's) power", of which he is (as he was even in his weakness) the personal embodiment.

**Jesus, the reality**

This was no less true in respect of the Law. As the writer would proceed to show his readers, the Priesthood, the Offerings, the Tabernacle – everything in fact to do with their revered Law – only made sense in terms of the Son's coming into the world. They were mere "patterns of things in the heavens", simply so many "figures of the true" (9:23,24). He was the reality which they prefigured, and thus, poetically speaking, the actual maker of them. But having come, he, in fulfilling them, also did away with them – himself remaining after them, as he was in the divine purpose conceived before them.

Such was the thought compressed for the writer into the psalm as quoted by him in 1:10-12. The Son had by himself definitively purged man's sin (verse 3), and was at that time awaiting the full inheritance of all things at the Father's right hand (1:2,13). The readers were blinded to this profound truth by their misguided concern with the Law which had by their Lord been both fulfilled and done away a full generation ago. Moses – the human mediator of the Law – with whom, as with the angels (the celestial mediators) they were so preoccupied, was himself no more than "a servant" in a great divine House, as yet incomplete, composed of men and women of all ages and origins, of which Christ as Son was Head, and (in the sense already explained) at the same time the builder for God (3:2-6). Their concern should be to see that they continued to be members of it as partakers of a truly "heavenly" calling (verses 1,6). For the Son, himself belonging to the heavenly order, and being now in fact seated in heaven at God's right hand, had through his disciples spoken to them "from heaven" (3:3; 12:25) – and that, if they could but see it, to the extent of bidding them be done with those earthly things which so engrossed them.

His Word, therefore, was final and absolute: to defy it was disastrous. "See" then, urged the writer, "that ye refuse not him that speaketh" (12:25). Of what criminal folly they were guilty if they decided not to heed his counsel!

# 4

## "THEM WHO DRAW BACK UNTO PERDITION"
*The fatal consequences of apostasy.*

WHEREVER we turn in Hebrews we find ourselves in the midst of discussion and debate. This point or that is being explained; familiar Scriptures are being interpreted anew; false notions are being corrected; contrary opinions are being anticipated and refuted before they can be put to use – in a word, the author is everywhere bent on enlightening his readers.

Yet nowhere does he regard the enlightenment of them as an end in itself. The opening section of the epistle is a case in point. There, upon the first available opportunity, we saw him break off to impress upon the readers the momentous practical consequences of what he had so far had to say. And the same phenomenon is everywhere to be met in the epistle. No sooner has an argument been advanced than a homiletic comment follows. Upon first sight, to us that comment seems in each case to interrupt the main flow of thought in the letter, and our natural tendency is to regard it as a digression. But let us on each occasion look at it a little more closely – and that with an eye once again to discovering its immediate relevance for the original readers *at that particular stage* in the development of the doctrinal thesis of the letter as a whole – and we find to our surprise that what seems to be a digression is anything but such. The truth is that the writer's intention is practical throughout, so that he is in fact pursuing his aim as much in these homiletic comments as in the purely exegetical portions of the letter which prove to us today so much more fascinating. He enlightens his readers only the better to stir them to action, so that where he seems at first to be moving away from the point, he is, if we can but see it, bringing it all the more bluntly home to them.

Another glance at his first warning confirms this. That warning has hitherto served us only as a help in following the arguments on which it is predicated. But now that we are aware of both the meaning and the ulterior aim of these arguments, we can with profit reverse the process, and allow them to lend fresh meaning to the warning itself.

It opened with an emphatic, "Therefore", which brought all this previous reasoning to bear upon his readers.

> "Therefore [said he] we ought to give the more earnest heed to the things which we have heard, lest at any time we should let them slip." (2:1)

Here, for the first time we note, he was disclosing his motive in writing his letter. It was to prevent his readers from drifting away from what they had "heard" when God "spoke" to them through His Son (1:1,2) – that is, from the Gospel. He would not have set out to do this unless he had had good reason for believing that they were thinking of abandoning their Christian hope. But they for their part would not have dreamt of so doing had they fully understood their position. It is this which he was now intent on making crystal clear to them.

## Consequences of rejecting the Gospel

He took their fanatical attachment to the Law as his starting point – since this was the very cause of their present peril. He would show them, in the light of what he had just had to say, that the very motive of that attachment – an awe of its authority and a fear of its threats of punishment for apostasy – had now become an even more powerful motive for adherence to the Gospel. Having demonstrated convincingly to them both the inferiority and the passing away of the Law, he would now point out to them without delay the greater enormity of disloyalty to the Gospel and the correspondingly excessive punishment which therefore

## "THEM WHO DRAW BACK UNTO PERDITION"

had to be – and would most certainly be – visited upon any who wantonly proved guilty of it. To quote the writer himself:

> "For if the word spoken by angels was stedfast, and every transgression and disobedience received a just recompence of reward; how shall we escape, if we neglect so great salvation?" (2:2,3)

The stress here fell upon the word "salvation". For one reason, because it announced a theme due for detailed treatment later, and for treatment in one of its aspects immediately – that is, the atoning work of Christ (verses 9-17; cf. 9:15, etc.). But there was another more urgent reason which concerned the warning itself; the readers, in forsaking Christ, were casting away salvation itself – and that a *"so great* salvation" – the measure of its greatness being that it was a salvation –

> "which at the first began to be spoken by the Lord, and was confirmed unto us by them that heard him; God also bearing them witness, both with signs and wonders, and with divers miracles, and gifts of the Holy Spirit, according to his own will." (2:3,4)

The qualifications cited were impressive. They disposed at once (in view of the foregoing arguments) of qualms as to the Gospel's authority, and also of doubts as to its authenticity. The original speaker of the divine message which they had received was none other than "the Lord" of 1:10 – that is, the abiding Son himself! As a guarantee of the fidelity with which it had been transmitted to them was the fact that those who preached it were this Lord's own immediate followers. But above and beyond that was the attestation of God Himself, stamping the message as "according to His own will". That is, the fundamental religious revolution effected by the advent of the Son was no chance consequence of his coming, but one specifically *willed* by God, as would later be shown in greater detail (cf. chapter 8). How foolish then, of the readers to refuse to give that "more earnest heed" which the nature of the new revelation necessitated! Small wonder that the author should thus summarily remind them of the inevitable consequences of their intended action, now that its true nature had been revealed to them. Their folly would bring them under the severest judgement of God.

**Lessons from the wilderness journey**

But, at this first stage, the writer could not yet afford to enlarge upon the matter. Sufficient for the moment to caution them in somewhat vague and general terms – "How shall we *escape* if we neglect so great salvation" – and to jolt them out of their complacency without dismaying them utterly. His choice of term, "escape", was just suggestive enough to make them scan the remainder of his letter all the more eagerly for an explanation of what precisely he meant by it. So for the moment he would deal with their "salvation" in more positive fashion, and allay other doubts and difficulties which the scandal of the Cross had inspired in them, thus preparing the way also for the full treatment later of the grand theme of the Lord's Priesthood (2:5-18). Yet in so doing he continued to bear his practical purpose in mind, and in choosing to compare Christ and Moses as Apostles, before comparing Christ and Aaron as High Priests, he made it possible for yet another homiletic discourse to be addressed to them just where it would be most timely. For the function of Moses being, like that of the whole Law, to serve as "a testimony of those things which were to be spoken after" – that is, to prefigure Christ – it was natural that the followers of the one – the Children of Israel redeemed at Passover – should likewise be regarded as an object lesson to the followers of the other – the Jewish Christians recently redeemed by the Sacrifice of Jesus (3:5). This mode of treatment also entailed, as we have seen (page 16), regarding the Promised Land as no more than a figure of the heavenly country to which the Christian's gaze is turned. How all this connected with the readers' doubts, difficulties, fears and intentions we have also had occasion to note (pp. 30-36), but one

## "THEM WHO DRAW BACK UNTO PERDITION"

further glance now at the writer's allegorical treatment of the wilderness journey serves to bring home to us with added force how essentially practical was the aim with which he wrote in the first place. Not without good reason did he ask with manifest allusion to the Old Testament records: "But with whom was he grieved forty years? was it not with them that had sinned, whose carcases fell in the wilderness?" (3:17). Here was more than a veiled hint: here was a deliberate appeal to the precedent set by their ancestors, and the plainest warning that "carcases" could yet again "fall in the wilderness" and exclusion from the coming Rest be once more the stern sentence of God.

But sentence for what? As we saw in our previous examination of the passage, a sentence of judgement against a deliberate hardening of the heart against God. When the first warning was sounded, severe though it was, the writer had to take account of the fact that his readers were largely ignorant of the implications of their calling. But the further he proceeded with his doctrinal argument and the more convincingly he vindicated his initial contention that God had in Christ put the Law away, clearly the more inexcusable became the desire on the part of the readers to adhere to the Law at all costs, even the cost of forsaking Christ. What might, at the outset, have been indulgently regarded as misguided zeal would now become wanton disobedience to the revealed will of God if persisted in any longer. Hence this particular solemn warning, at this particular point: the author was imploring his readers, whom he feared to be by now incensed at his reasoning and the conclusions to which it led, to listen to him to the end – not to close their ears wilfully to what he had to tell them, but to "hear God's voice", lest the fate of their fathers became theirs also. The "sin" which was so deceitfully assailing them was that of apostasy. Well may we marvel at his tact, his human understanding, his choice of the psychological moment to sound this ominous warning – and that in the language of their own revered Scriptures.

**Paying heed**

As we move onwards to the next warning in the series which occur at regular intervals in the epistle, we need constantly to remember that the author was, from this point on, thinking and writing in terms primarily of a *deliberate, calculated* refusal to pay "the more earnest heed" which he had enjoined at the outset. It was with apostasy persisted in against the readers' better (for it was now a truly enlightened) judgement that he was dealing in the subsequent warnings which we shall now proceed to examine. If we forget that fact, we run the risk inevitably of misunderstanding his meaning and applying his words to circumstances which are not necessarily parallel to those which he envisaged.

The next warning in the series was not only lengthier and more complicated, but, as by now we would expect, also more explicit and more severe. It forms a transition between the announcement of Jesus as "called of God an high priest after the order of Melchisedec" (5:10) and the detailed exposition of that matter from 6:20 onwards. Some of its terms are strange to us, so that to understand them aright we need to take extra care to fit the passage solidly into the framework of the epistle as a whole.

The author began with a rebuke. He had, up to this point, been ceaselessly engaged in explaining matters which, if new, were thus to the shame and discredit of his readers. Their hearing had lost its sensitivity, become slothful (cf. 6:12), so that the matters about which he wished to talk to them were well-nigh beyond their comprehension (verse 11). They had a capacity for teaching others and the experience now to do so, but being through their own neglect unpractised in the understanding of the Scriptures and lacking in discernment, they were instead in need of being themselves instructed – his letter being witness (5:12-14).

Now this rebuke would not have made sense unless the matters with which the author would shortly proceed

## "THEM WHO DRAW BACK UNTO PERDITION"

to deal were part of that "strong meat", to assimilate which they would never have proved capable without his help. Hence his significant words of encouragement:

"Therefore *leaving* the principles of the doctrine of Christ, let us *go on* unto perfection (i.e., maturity, cf. 5:14) ... And this will we do, if God permit." (6:1,3)

He thus wished to lead them onwards. But the words that follow make it clear that they themselves – and we have already had proof enough of this – were contemplating turning *backwards:*

"This will we do [said he], if God permit. *For* it is impossible for those who were once enlightened ... if they shall *fall away*, to renew them again unto repentance." (6:3-6)

These last solemn words, taken in conjunction with the rebuke which precedes them, make it clear that the readers were poised midway between going forward with his help, and going backward if they refused that help. This arose from the fact that to themselves they were Jews first and Christians next, rather than Christians first and Jews next. It was their *Christianity* which was in danger, and that precisely because they were contemplating a step back to Judaism which would have ended their career – as well they realized – as *Christians*. It is important to take careful note of this fact, for the language used by the writer can otherwise be misunderstood. He talks of leaving (i.e., moving on from) "the principles of (the doctrine of) Christ".

### The principles of Christ

What does that term mean? Does it mean the elements of Judaism? If so, in what need did his readers stand, being Jews, of having that particular foundation laid again? Clearly none. Does it mean precisely the same thing as "the first principles of the oracles of God" in 5:12? If so, why the change in phraseology, slight though it be? Different words must stand for different notions here, and to be able to understand both terms we need to be able to distinguish what is peculiar to each. Does it then mean the foundation truths of

Christianity – those elements in Christianity which would at their conversion be distinctive for them as men already steeped in Judaism? The terms of the warning which follows make it clear that this is the only possible answer, for it envisages a "falling away" which is followed by a desire to be "renewed again". Now a Christian poised, as these men were, between a going forward to Christian perfection, and a going back to what had been his before conversion – who chose the lesser in preference to the greater – might very well regret the decision shortly afterwards. Could such a man be "renewed again unto repentance"? *That was the crux.* The "laying again", at issue here, was not of the foundations of Judaism, but of *Christianity*. The warning here sounded was to men who were on the brink of a grave decision. The writer was intent on pointing out to them that the decision was not only grave, but *irrevocable* – as irrevocable as that of the spies who tasted of the fruit of the land, chose not to enter, and were refused entry when their folly dawned upon them (Numbers 13:1-33; 14:40-45). "It is *impossible*", said he, "for those who were once (i.e., *"once for all"*, cf. Hebrews 9:27,28) enlightened, and have tasted of the heavenly gift, and were made partakers of the Holy Spirit, and have tasted the good word of God, and the powers of the world to come, if they shall fall away to renew them again unto repentance" (6:4-6; cf. 12:16,17).

The succession of significant expressions produces a grand rhetorical effect. They who had been so richly endowed, could they, in spurning what had been endowed on them, expect to receive it back if later they relented? "Impossible", came the blunt, heart-chilling answer, calculated to make any falterer hesitate before making his choice.

Here, then, the writer was – as everywhere in the epistle – at grips with Christian Jews, tempted to return to Judaism. They had failed to continue in that understanding of the oracles of God which had been theirs when they saw in Christ the fulfilment of Old Testament prophecy concerning the coming of the

## "THEM WHO DRAW BACK UNTO PERDITION"

Messiah (5:12). They had not graduated to that grasp of typology which by now should have been theirs, and which, if they had possessed it, would have not necessitated the writer's warning that the things about which he was now going to talk would be things "hard to be uttered" (verse 11). Their present dilemma was thus the fruit of their own neglect. But let them not think that even their basic endowment as Christians – "the principles of Christ" – could twice become theirs. No. Enlightenment is "once for all" – an unrepeatable process. "Laying again the foundation of repentance from dead works, and of faith toward God, of the doctrine of baptisms, and of laying on of hands, and of resurrection of the dead, and of eternal judgment" – this was not something which could take place more than once (6:1,2). When they had been converted they had acknowledged the need, though Jews after the flesh, to repent from "dead works" (i.e., from their offences against the Law – cf. 9:14,15) and to accept in faith (Acts 3:25,26) the offer of free pardon which God had made in Christ in annulment of their condemned state as sinners (6:1). They had acknowledged in true Christian baptism the antitype of all other washings under the Law, and in formal association with a crucified Christ the antitype of the laying on of hands in the ritual of sacrifice and a symbol of the identification of themselves with him and his. That beginning made, they had pledged themselves thereafter to live as awaiting the resurrection of the dead and an eventual call to undergo an eternal judgement.

### Going back – not an option

Could a return by them to the type, and a forsaking of the antitype, be made with impunity? No; this same factor of eternal judgement forbade it. Any of them guilty of such folly and rebellion, however sorry afterwards, would find sorrow unavailing. For what would their act be – that is, the act which *they, in their peculiar circumstances*, would thus commit? The author gave them the answer:

"It is impossible ... to renew them again unto repentance; seeing they crucify to themselves the Son of God afresh, and put him to an open shame." (6:4-6)

That is, it would be the forsaking not of a mere man – but of the *Son* himself! of him whose greatness has been made so plain to them at the outset; a shaming of him whose sitting at the right hand of God was his glory. And that an *open* shame! Why "open"? Firstly because, given the circumstances, their act of apostasy would be overt – a matter of public knowledge among their unbelieving brethren. And secondly, because, as we shall shortly have reason to see, it would have in any case to be accompanied, for the satisfaction of those unbelieving brethren, by a public renunciation of their Christianity – a public endorsement therefore, of the legitimacy of the Crucifixion – in brief, a repudiation of Christ as an imposter.

Could God, who had so richly blessed them, stand by unmoved by so monstrous an act of treachery? If they denied Him the spiritual harvest to which He was entitled, what could they expect, with the precedent of their fathers of every generation as an object lesson before their eyes? As the writer put it, with a deft change of figure:

"For the earth which drinketh in the rain that cometh oft upon it, and bringeth forth herbs meet for them by whom it is dressed, receiveth blessing from God: but that which beareth thorns and briers is rejected, and is nigh unto cursing; whose end is to be burned." (verses 7,8)

## Privilege brings responsibility

He would not, however, end on so severe a note, sound it though he had to; so he proceeded next to plead with them in words of encouragement rather than of menace. But the menace had to be sounded. God is not mocked: the greater men's privileges, the greater their responsibilities, and thus the heavier their punishment if they prove unfaithful. Such was the lesson which the writer would have his readers learn.

The severity of the language here was thus unavoidable, and that, we note, precisely because it was prompted by a peculiar kind of sin – not a sin of mere weakness, but a defiant spurning of what had at first been received from God with joy, and had proved a source of happiness and help for long years since. And that a spurning without shame, and without remorse – at least in the first instance.

Yet later there came language even more terrifying, and explicit – as indeed we might expect, since it came after demonstration, even more convincing, of the power of the Cross of Christ and of the fact that it was by the personal decision of the Father that the Law had become inoperative. It was also language which took account of additional factors in the case of the readers. Already the writer had urged them to stand together and lend each to the other help and encouragement:

"Take heed, brethren, lest there be in any of you an evil heart of unbelief, in departing from the living God. But exhort one another daily, while it is called Today; lest any of you be hardened through the deceitfulness of sin." (3:12,13)

## "The day approaching"

His doctrinal arguments all completed, he returned once more to this same subject, but only to deal with it much more fully. For beside the good example which could be set, there were bad examples which were already being given. The process of drift had begun, and some among these Hebrews had already taken the step of apostasy. His counsel was therefore twofold. On the one hand:

"Let us draw near with a true heart in full assurance of faith ... let us hold fast the profession of our hope without wavering ... and let us consider one another to provoke unto love and to good works." (10:22-24)

And on the other:

> "Not forsaking the assembling of ourselves together, as the manner of some is; but exhorting one another: and so much the more, as ye see the day approaching." (verse 25)

And at that point he launched out into his most menacing warning yet against apostasy. Why should it be at this point? It had clearly some connection with some "day" of great moment to him and his readers. What "day" was this? The context suggests either the day when the Jewish War would actually break out, complicating even further the already delicate position in which the readers found themselves, or a day which had been given to them in some kind of ultimatum issued by their unbelieving brethren – a day of fateful choice. They could quail before the prospect and turn traitor to the Gospel, or they could stand shoulder to shoulder, and lend each other strength of will to "hold fast" the "profession" of their faith. In such a desperate situation only those too weak to endure the trial of their faith would be rash enough to stand apart from the others. Those well able to endure would be only too eager to help the faltering. Thus separation of themselves from other Christians was fraught with peril – hence the exhortation not to forsake the assembling of themselves together, but to exhort one another, and so much the more as they saw the Day approaching.

## Warning of judgement

So much for them. But the thought of those whose reason for forsaking the assemblies was a wish to return to Judaism at once prompted the warning:

> "For if we sin wilfully after that we have received the knowledge of the truth, there remaineth no more sacrifice for sins, but a certain fearful looking for of judgment and fiery indignation, which shall devour the adversaries." (verses 26,27)

The same mention of fire as before, we note; but also the same idea of *wilful* sin, which, in the context of the epistle as a whole, meant calculated apostasy, the deliberate turning of one's back on Christ. And how calculated, and how deliberate, the words that followed show to us:

"He that despised Moses' law died without mercy under two or three witnesses: of how much sorer punishment, suppose ye, shall he be thought worthy, who hath trodden underfoot the Son of God, and hath counted the blood of the covenant, wherewith he was sanctified, an unholy thing, and hath done despite unto the Spirit of grace?" (verses 28,29)

Now, clearly, the act of forsaking Christ, here envisaged, was not the apathetic drifting away of the lukewarm, but, as the very writing of the letter is witness, the express choice, by zealots, of Moses in preference to Christ. That is, the forsaking of the Christian assemblies was *ipso facto* a return to those of the synagogue. Given the situation existing at the time, can it be imagined that the synagogue authorities would re-admit a renegade Christian Jew without prior interview, and without receiving reassurances that his faith in the Crucified One was now dead? That is, transfer from the Christian gathering to the Synagogue would automatically be accompanied by a formal public repudiation by the Christian Jew of his Christianity. *That*, then: that is what the author meant by the expression, "if we sin *wilfully*"! The apostate Christian Jew would solemnly repudiate in public the claims of Christ – thus treading underfoot the Son of God – the *Son* of chapter 1! He would endorse the judgement passed on Jesus by the Synagogue and disown the Cross – thus counting the blood of the Covenant wherewith he was sanctified, an unholy thing. He would explain the divine attestation of the truth of the message preached by the disciples of Jesus as the work of Beelzebub (cf. Matthew 12:24-32) – thus doing despite to the Spirit of grace. Apostasy to the Law, during its period of validity meant death without mercy (Deuteronomy 17:2-7). "Of how much sorer punishment" was that man worthy who could thus wilfully prove traitor to Christ! For him there was no forgiveness possible either in this world or in that to come – "for we know him", said the writer, "that hath said, Vengeance belongeth unto me, I will recompense, saith the Lord". And again, "The Lord shall judge his people" (Hebrews 10:30,31). Then, finally, weighing his words most carefully, he added the awful comment: "It is a fearful thing to fall into the hands of the living God."

## Prospects of life or death

Such was the prospect which the readers had to reckon with in wishing to "fall away". More than ever the need would be obvious to them to "go on" instead, "to perfection". With timely words of cheer the writer at once proceeded to urge them anew to do so – reminding them of their past steadfastness, of the need for patience, and finally of the certainty of the Lord's coming, not only as Judge, but as Saviour (verses 32-37). The witness of the prophet was, "Now the just shall *live* by faith". But the converse was also true – "If any man draw back, my soul shall have *no pleasure* in him" (verse 38).

Which way would the readers choose?

"We [said the writer making their minds up for them] are not of them who draw back unto perdition; but of them that have faith to the saving of the soul."

(verse 39)

If they boldly added their voices to his, then the prospect before them was not that of eternal death, but rather that of the joy of life everlasting, and of entry into "the city of the living God" – the abode of "the spirits of just men made perfect" (12:23).

# 5

## "FOR THE SUFFERING OF DEATH"
*The indispensability of the Cross.*

NOT a subject is treated in the main body of our epistle without there being some account taken of it, if only implicitly in the majestic statement with which the letter opens. The writer was clearly resolved that, even if no more than this section of his letter were read, at least a bold profession would have been made of faith in those matters which, for his readers, had of late become the subject of such serious doubt or concern.

**The pre-eminence of Christ**
Such was manifestly the case with his forthright assertion that the Son, "when he had by himself purged our sins, sat down on the right hand of the Majesty on high" (1:3).

The attention subsequently devoted to these two great matters – the sacrifice and the exaltation of the Son – can only mean that the readers were succumbing to the view, so zealously preached by their unbelieving brethren, that Jesus had been no more than a bogus Messiah, seeing that he had died so ignominious a death. To this the writer here made the summary rejoinder that the same Jesus who had died in shame, had thereafter been raised to glory. Deny it as his readers might, such were the unquestionable facts. Yet how subtle and tactful was his affirmation of them! How masterly to couch it in each case in Scriptural terms. In declaring Jesus to have "sat down at the right hand of the Majesty on high", who could he be proclaiming him to be but the Messiah? And where lay the grounds for the gibes and taunts of their orthodox brethren, seeing that the death of Jesus had, after all, been not a punishment for treason, nor simply a tragic martyrdom, but an act of atonement – a *purging* of sin?

But confident assertions were not enough on their own. The author needed also to vindicate them, and that in the same way as he had made them – in Scriptural language.

He chose to do so, we note, in reverse order, dealing first with the glory, and only next with the shame. This order of treatment was dictated by his overriding aim: his first need, as now we are in a position to appreciate, was to affirm the pre-eminence of the Son, since it was this which was the secret of Christ's claim upon the loyalty of Jewish believers. But, that first task accomplished, there remained yet another – one made all the more difficult, in one way, by the success of the first – that of reconciling this pre-eminence with the undoubted abasement which had gone before it, and which was now a matter of such heart-searching to the readers.

## The creation of man

For the writer, Psalm 8 resolved the enigma. This psalm is a meditation upon the Creation story, so to appreciate its message – and thus its value for the author of Hebrews – we need first to take careful note, both of the setting, and of the precise terms, of the Genesis account of man's creation.

First the setting. There is no mistaking the fact, when the order in which the facts are related is taken carefully into account, that Genesis intends us to see the formation of man as not only the culminating, but also the crowning, act of Creation – and this at the same time, paradoxically, as it presents man to us as essentially part and parcel of the animal kingdom. Not until He had completed the calling into being of the whole material order, and also of the hierarchy of the animal world, did God, finally, announce His intention to create man. And these were the significant terms in which He did so:

## "FOR THE SUFFERING OF DEATH"

"God said, Let us make man in our image, after our likeness: and let them have dominion over the fish of the sea, and over the fowl of the air, and over the cattle, and over all the earth, and over every creeping thing that creepeth upon the earth." (Genesis 1:26) Finally, to this expression of intention we find these further words of comment added by the writer of Genesis:

"So God created man in his own image, in the image of God created he him; male and female created he them. And God blessed them, and God said unto them, Be fruitful, and multiply, and replenish the earth, and subdue it, and have dominion ..."

(verses 27,28)

There is a majestic sweep about these statements: as the Psalmist was so quick to perceive, they were concerned with much more than the terms of reference of just the first human pair. Firstly, they assigned to the entire human family – and not to Adam and Eve only – and that throughout all time, a fundamental purpose in life – that of being like God. Secondly, on that same basis, they announced man's ultimate function to be to attain to sovereignty over *everything* that had been made before him, and not simply over the earth and its denizens. Thus, though physically no better than any other animal, man was meant to be much more than just an animal. Being the culmination of Creation, he was destined by God to graduate to total supremacy over it as His own vicegerent.

The thought is staggering, and immeasurably more so when we take into account man's minuteness in the face of the vastness of Creation. The Psalmist was moved by it to cry in awe:

"When I consider thy heavens, the work of thy fingers, the moon and the stars, which thou hast ordained; what is man, that thou art mindful of him? and the son of man, that thou visitest him? For thou hast made him a little lower than the angels, and hast crowned him with glory and honour."

(Psalm 8:3-5)

"Thou hast made him a little lower than the angels" – here was the certainty of history, the facts of Genesis being witness: God in thus determining the purpose and end of man's life had virtually exalted him, there and then, to the rank of the angels! But in the certainty of the past the Psalmist saw warrant also for certainty as to the future – a certainty so unassailable that he could speak of that future as though it were already fact. Not only could he look back and say, "Thou hast made him a little lower than the angels", but he could also look forward and boldly proclaim:

"[Thou] hast crowned him with glory and honour. Thou madest him to have dominion over the works of thy hands; thou hast put *all* things under his feet."

(Psalm 8:5,6)

And all this with not a mention of man's Fall! Why not? Clearly because, for the Psalmist, the Fall, though as real a fact of history as the Creation itself, in no way invalidated the original divine intention – "Let us make man in our image ... and let them have dominion". These words set in operation a process which would not end until they had realized themselves absolutely – such was the Psalmist's conviction, and the ground of his hope.

## The Fall

But did that mean that the Fall was, after all, of no moment whatsoever? Emphatically not. In the nature of things God could not ignore it, and, in using the psalm to support his argument, the writer to the Hebrews had no intention of leaving out of account the complications caused by the Fall. Rather was the contrary the case as we shall very soon see. But his use of it would immediately make two things very clear to his readers. The one was that the angels, besides having established an order which was destined to serve only for a while and afterwards be put away, were not even to exercise control over the one order which would abide! The other – bearing closely on the case of the Son – was that temporary inferiority to the angels did not in itself preclude an ultimate attainment to a rank superior to theirs.

The psalm was quoted – and with manifest aptness – specifically to prove that "unto the *angels* hath God not put in subjection the world to come, whereof we speak". No: the testimony of the psalm was categorical – not for angels, but for *man* was that honour reserved; man who had in the first place been made lower than they.

"Thou crownedst him with glory and honour, and didst set him over the works of thy hands: thou hast put all things in subjection under his feet." (2:7,8)

"*All* things". No question here of the allotment of control over some things to angels, and others to man – *all* was to be subjected to man and to man alone: "For in that he put all in subjection under him, he left *nothing* that is not put under him" (verse 8). Language could not be plainer.

But why was the author so dogmatic? Need we ask? Never, as we have abundantly seen, did he affirm facts for the mere sake of doing so. In thus insisting on the limits to the power of the angels, he was bent on heightening not the power of mankind in the aggregate, but that of one man among men in particular. The issue was still – 'The angels, or *the Son*?' After the Creation came the Fall, as he and his readers knew, so that for the original divine intention to remain valid in the changed circumstances caused by the Fall, and thus for it to realize itself despite the Fall, some extraordinary transformation in man's situation had of necessity to come about.

The author's point was that that transformation had in fact already come about – and this in perfect accord both with Genesis and the psalm. In the face of this breathtaking language, used in each about man in the mass, one could indeed only reply, pathetically, bitterly, hopelessly even, with man's black record taken into account:

"But now we see not yet *all things put under* him." But how different was the situation when that language was construed Christologically! When in the term "man" the name "Jesus" was espied, how luminous did everything suddenly become! Despair was forthwith transmuted into hope.

## Christ's dominion

Why? Well, where God had said, "Let us make man in our image", could it not now be said, "The Son was the effulgence of His glory, the express image – the perfect replica in flesh – of what God is"? Unless Jesus had come in flesh – that is, been in the full sense a man, even though the Son, and thus been himself, like all men, inferior to the angels at the outset – the divine word, "Let us make man in our image", could not have thus realized itself as God intended. But now it had. So, consequently, the divine mandate – "Have dominion" – if unable to be realized in *all* men, could still be realized in this unique One, who alone was worthy to receive it. And, moreover – though as yet only in part – it *had* in fact, been realized, for (as the author had already asked) "to which of the angels said he at any time, Sit on my right hand, until I make thine enemies thy footstool?" (1:13). Not to angels, but to the Son only, God had said this. But in saying it, God had raised the Son from earth to heaven, elevated him from the realm of flesh to that of spirit, and assured him in the act of doing so, that all would eventually be put "in subjection under *his* feet"! Whereas, then, the divine intention had been consistently frustrated in all others, in Jesus it had actually come to fulfilment. In terms of him it at last made sense; so much so, that it could with truth be said that it had been originally conceived in terms only of his eventual coming, and that it had thus, ultimately, envisaged him alone. It became obvious here, once again, that it was through him that God had made the ages, and that he, in his own person, bore (as he still bears) "all things" to their divinely appointed goal (verses 2,3).

Thus where the despairing comment, "But we see not yet *all things* put under man", seemed so justifiable, the joyous rejoinder could also now be made, "But we behold Jesus ..."

The verb "behold" was chosen with consummate aptness, for vision – spiritual vision – was needed before the readers could realize that in the heavenly realm the divine purpose was fulfilling itself in Jesus, despite his absence, and was moving towards its final and absolute realization. In attaining to that realm Jesus, unique amongst men, had *already* become "crowned with glory and honour", and was now only awaiting the moment for the full inheritance of absolute supremacy over "all things" intended for him from the very beginning of Creation.

**Why the Cross?**

But did that mean that the divine intention never envisaged more than him? Such was the obvious problem raised by this Christological interpretation of the psalm. And there still remained also, for the readers, the stubborn fact of the Cross. Granted that the present "glory" of the Son offset its shame, what had been the point, or need, of the Cross in the first place?

The author could now give a confident answer. For whereas the Fall had caused no alteration in the divine intention – "Let us make man in our image ... and let them have dominion" – it had inevitably entailed a radical change in the means of its realization. Where the intention of God had *included*, the Fall had in its turn *excluded*, the whole human family. So the author was now able to adapt, to the problem here raised, his own previously stated formula – "When he had by himself *purged* our sins, [he] sat down on the right hand of the Majesty on high".

"We behold Jesus [said he], who was made a little lower than the angels, because of the suffering of death crowned with glory and honour, so that he by

the grace of God should taste death for *every* man."
(2:9)

That is, the glory to which Jesus had attained, far from being incompatible with his death, was the direct consequence of it, that death being a death to re-include humanity within the scope of the divine purpose.

Here was fresh light indeed on the death of Jesus. Before the advent of sin the divine intention had envisaged him as its perfect expression. But after that advent, argued the writer, it required him to be, in addition, the One to purge sin. Otherwise it could not realize itself in others besides him. Now sin being what it is – the seed of death – this of necessity required him to die. Not only had he to be a man anyway, but he had also, in being a man, to be a *mortal* man – a man *capable* of dying – a man, that is, to the uttermost. In brief, he had to be as really and as fully made in the image and after the likeness of *fallen* man, as in the image of God Himself.

## Son of God and Son of Man

Was his humanity, or even his death, then, as some readers were now inclined to think, a denial of his claims? By no means: the very reverse was true. It was precisely because he was the Son that he was required to undergo death. He, the Son of God, was also destined to be the representative of men – the Son of Man of Psalm 8 – the microcosm of a new regenerated humanity. But humanity being in the first place unregenerate, it could become regenerate, in and through him, only on condition that he first became fully one with it. That was the fundamental truth of which the readers had failed to take account:

"For [said the writer] it became him (i.e., God), for whom are all things, and by whom are all things, in bringing many sons unto glory, to make the captain of their salvation perfect through sufferings." (verse 10)

That is, the Son was a Saviour because he was himself first saved: he himself was "made perfect", as a forerunner, as a pioneer, as the Firstborn.

## "FOR THE SUFFERING OF DEATH"

The writer thus regarded the Son as inextricably bound up with humanity at large. As he put it:

"Both he that sanctifieth (i.e., Jesus), and they who are sanctified, are all of one." (verse 11)

This solidarity – first in nature, then in destiny – this oneness – explained why Jesus should not be ashamed to call sinners his brethren. Because they went to make up the "many sons" destined like himself to attain at last to glory, he could freely acknowledge them as such there and then, "Saying; I will declare thy name unto my *brethren*, in the midst of the church will I sing praise unto thee". He, in his human weakness, knew himself to be as dependent upon God as they were, so that he, like them, could say also, "I will put my trust in him". And, lastly, with the vision before him of the ultimate sharing of glory with them, he could add yet again:

"Behold I and the children which God hath given me." (verses 12,13)

His solidarity with humanity could not have been more clearly attested. Yet to make it doubly certain that the readers understood it, and its implications, the author added:

"Forasmuch then as the children are partakers of flesh and blood, he also himself likewise took part of the same; that through death he might destroy him that had the power of death ..." (verse 14)

Jesus was born, in effect, to die – and that sacrificially, so as to purge men's sins. Had this not been so – had he come instead in angelic nature and so not been capable of death – there would have been no hope for the rest of mankind; "but he took on him the seed of Abraham" – that is, he fully participated in human nature, mortal though it was as a result of Adam's Fall, in order to be able in his own person, by dying, to reconcile all humanity to God (verse 16).

### A perfect answer

The author's case was thus the perfect answer to his readers' qualms. They saw in the Crucifixion a stumbling block: he replied by declaring it to be the means judged best by God Himself – by Him who is the first and efficient Cause of all things! – of achieving the purpose which He had conceived before the world was. The One Son was, in his own person, to be "many" sons: that is, he had of necessity as Saviour to be identified with them that they might in turn be identifiable with him. This meant that because they, according to the righteous sentence of God after the Fall, had to die, so had he, that they might as it were die in him, and so in turn be raised with him to glory. This amazing process of sanctification from sin was "by the *grace* of God" – that is, not something due to man, but a free gift of God. Would the readers, out of obstinate attachment to false ideas, be foolish enough to spurn it – be so rash as to "neglect so great salvation"? – that was the thought which the reasoning would inevitably raise in their minds as they read it.

And they would also see further significance in the writer's words. Isaiah 53 would inevitably be recalled to their minds: suffering which they were disposed to regard as incompatible with the exaltation of the Son would once again take on its proper meaning. They would see themselves to have been healed by his stripes. And more than that: they were quailing before the prospect of martyrdom – but because he had broken the power of diabolos, they would now see that, provided they were faithful, he could raise them to glory as he himself had been raised to glory by God. Furthermore, they in their dilemma, felt forsaken – but now, if they could but realize it, the humanity which they wished to count as a reproach against Christ, was the guarantee of his abiding sympathy with them. He had "suffered" death, "tasted" death, known human anguish experimentally, and thus acquired a sympathy with them which remained with him in his exaltation. Without that prior experience his glory would have spelt no immediate benefit to his human brethren in their own trials. Therefore, argued the writer, it had been right and proper – it had been absolutely essential

## "FOR THE SUFFERING OF DEATH"

– that the Son should have been at first made just like all the many sons whom he came to save:

"Wherefore in all things it behoved him to be made like unto his brethren, that he might be a merciful and faithful high priest in things pertaining to God, to make reconciliation for the sins of the people. For in that he himself hath suffered being tempted, he is able to succour them that are tempted."     (2:17,18)

Here were two topics which clearly needed much ampler treatment – the High Priesthood and the atoning work of the Son. They would most certainly receive that treatment later – for the readers' difficulties were the fruit of a zealous attachment to the established Aaronic priesthood on the one hand, and to the sacred ritual of animal sacrifice on the other. In using such language the writer was thus giving notice that he would reconcile his reasoning here with the Law as a whole. But up to this point he had been intent on keeping the whole discussion on the purely human plane. Man is the being appointed to eventual lordship over Creation; man alone is responsible for sin: therefore it was in man himself that the scheme of salvation had to be brought out.

Thus, said the writer, in effect, all the needs of the situation had been met in Jesus – the Son of God, and Son of Man. If only his sufferings were seen in this light all else would assuredly fall into place. To show how true this was – and that in terms of the Law itself – was therefore the task which next lay before him.

# 6

## "CROWNED WITH GLORY AND HONOUR"
*The Saviour exalted to priesthood.*

AS is by now obvious, the author was, in his second chapter, concerned with the Cross. Yet not exclusively so, as the conclusion of the chapter clearly proves. For while, for his Jewish Christian readers, his apology for the humanity and sufferings of the Son was meant to be the perfect answer to their misgivings about the Crucifixion, he had throughout, unknown to them, emphasised that humanity with an eye as much to the ultimate exaltation of the Son as to the prior humiliation which for them now seemed to have ruled that exaltation out. The first hint of this was given in 2:17 with the treatment, for the first time – and as yet only summarily – of the grand distinctive theme of the epistle – the High Priesthood of Christ. He would have them know that the sufferings of the Son had wonderfully qualified him for further saving work on their behalf.

"Wherefore [said he], holy brethren, partakers of the heavenly calling, *consider* the Apostle and High Priest of our profession, Christ Jesus." (3:1)

### A great High Priest

Immediately upon this plea there followed that consideration of Moses and Jesus as Apostles of God which led naturally on to the construing of the wilderness journey as an allegory of the Christian life (cf pp. 60,61). But back in due course came the writer to the topic of priesthood. It was futile said he, in effect, for the readers to think that their inner motives for apostasy could be concealed: the thoughts and intents of the hearts were all known to God, and nothing in them could escape the divine scrutiny (4:12,13). How much wiser, therefore, for them to come for succour to him who knew them through and through, and who, knowing them, knew also their need, and who, what was more, was able to satisfy that need to the full.

"Seeing then [pleaded the writer] that we have a great high priest, that is passed into the heavens, Jesus the Son of God, let us hold fast our profession." (verse 14)

Every word in this plea had been carefully selected. This was not only *a* High Priest, but a *great* High Priest, for he had passed not into the symbolic, but into the *actual*, presence of God. Moreover, human though he had first been to the full – as his name Jesus so expressively reminded the readers – he was also, as had been again so signally proved at the outset, God's Son! "Let us", then, said the writer, "hold fast our profession". And thereupon he made yet another emphatic assertion of the Son's capacity for sympathy:

"For we have not an high priest which cannot be touched with the feeling of our infirmities; but was in all points tempted like as we are, yet without sin. Let us therefore come boldly unto the throne of grace, that we may obtain mercy, and find grace to help in time of need." (verses 15,16)

This language would fairly take the readers' breath away when first they heard it. Not only did it announce that they had a *different* High Priest from the one held in such high esteem by their non-Christian brethren; but it also called upon them to make personally what had by the Law been marked out as the prerogative of the consecrated priests alone, and that on certain rare and exceptional occasions only – that is, a direct approach to the throne of God. But this they were now free to do. No longer need dread of the consequences deter them – that throne was now a true mercy-seat, a throne not only of holiness but also of grace. There was mercy extended for their misdeeds in the past, and help obtainable for their need in the present.

Or so, the author affirmed. For, let us never forget, he had for them to justify all his contentions, and it is not hard to imagine with what impatience some of them would by now be awaiting his Scriptural proof in support of them.

## The role of the Priest

There was no lack of such proof in actual fact, and they would with but little further delay be presented with it. But the better to ensure that they would feel its full power when it came, the author needed first to remind them, with Aaron as example, what precisely the Priest's role was.

It was that of mediator between God and man with a view to healing the breach between them caused by the Fall:

> "For every high priest taken from among men is ordained for men in things pertaining to God, that he may offer both gifts and sacrifices for sins." (5:1)

Now no angel had been selected to do this work for the very good reason that angels were, by nature, incapable of the requisite sympathetic insight into human experience and frailty. So, in contrast to them, Aaron, being "taken from among men", had automatically the capacity for sympathy essential to his office. He could "have compassion on the ignorant, and on them that are out of the way; for that he himself was compassed with infirmity" (verse 2).

But there, alas, lay a grievous complication. By reason of that very infirmity which qualified him to experience this compassion, Aaron had, "as for the people, *so also for himself*, to offer for sins" (verses 1-3). Thus there was never any question of his arrogating to himself the functions of priesthood: God alone could confer them on him:

> "No man taketh this honour unto himself, but he that is called of God, as was Aaron." (verse 4)

Now the novel news – and that, of course, Scriptural news – which the author would at this juncture bring to his readers' notice, was that not only Aaron, but Jesus also, had been called to priesthood. But in advancing his proof of this fact he would, once again, advance it not for the mere sake of doing so, but in strict pursuance of his polemical purpose. His ulterior object was to prove that Aaron had actually made way as Priest for Jesus – that is, that Jesus had actually rendered the Aaronic priesthood obsolete and so redundant. For the attainment of that object he had, we now note, made the most careful preparation when stating that Jesus, though "in all points tempted like as we are" had been so tempted "*without sin*". This inevitably meant that there was no need for him, as there had been for Aaron, "to offer for sins" of his own.

For all concerned in the present crisis this difference was crucial. Clad in his official vestments Aaron had indeed been an imposing sight. But the fact remained that before ever he had been permitted to don them, he had first to wash himself symbolically free of sin; and even after so doing he had to wear, beneath his glittering external robes, a simple coat of white linen – the perfect symbol of innocence. Yet it was a *symbol* and no more. There was no counterpart to it in the actual moral condition of Aaron – and that sad fact had received full publicity during – of all times – his consecration to office; for the very basis of that consecration had been a sacrifice for sin! (Leviticus 8:1-14).

Thus clearer proof could not be wanted of the fact that, as Priest, Aaron had been a purely symbolic personage, and so had served only as a prefigurement of One who was to come, One in whose person all that was mere symbol in him should become at last a concrete reality. Of that One, therefore, the writer would now speak expressly.

## The Priest – symbol of moral and physical perfection

At this point, however, we need once again to remind ourselves that perfect familiarity on the part of the readers with the facts of the Old Testament would be assumed by the writer. Such is manifestly the case in the pointed statement that Aaron had, "as for the people, so also for himself, to offer for sins" (5:3). But, if we are to appreciate the author's next arguments to the full, we need to realize in addition that in the Old Testament, as the readers would again be aware, Aaron was a symbol not only of moral, but also of *physical* perfection. The same man who had to purge himself of sin by washing, and to conceal his sin by being robed in white, had also as an essential qualification for office to be without all outward *physical* blemish. The Law was explicit:

"And the LORD spake unto Moses, saying, Speak unto Aaron, saying, Whosoever he be of thy seed in their generations that hath any blemish, let him not approach to offer the bread of his God. For whatsoever man he be that hath a blemish, he shall not approach: a blind man, or a lame, or he that hath a flat nose, or any thing superfluous, or a man that is brokenfooted, or brokenhanded, or crookbackt, or a dwarf, or that hath a blemish in his eye, or be scurvy, or scabbed, or hath his stones broken; no man that hath a blemish of the seed of Aaron the priest shall come nigh to offer the offerings of the LORD made by fire: he hath a blemish; he shall not come nigh to offer the bread of his God." (Leviticus 21:16-21)

Now here was a paradox indeed. Aaron had been appointed a Priest because, through being in every respect a man, he could sympathise fully with his brethren; yet if this freedom from physical blemish was in its turn to have any point at all, it was also his function to represent One who would be free of such blemish not in symbol only, but also in actual fact! – that is One who would, in nature, be *immune* to death. Now this, of course, Aaron, as a sinner, could never himself be: yet, as a symbolic figure, he had nevertheless to appear to be so. This was made possible, we find, by a stringent ruling of the Law.

"The LORD said unto Moses, Speak unto the priests the sons of Aaron, and say unto them, There shall none be defiled for the dead among his people ...

And he that is the high priest among his brethren, upon whose head the anointing oil was poured, and that is consecrated to put on the garments, shall not uncover his head, nor rend his clothes; neither shall he go in to any dead body, nor defile himself for his father, or for his mother; neither shall he go out of the sanctuary, nor profane the sanctuary of his God; for the crown of the anointing oil of his God is upon him: I am the LORD."  (verses 1-12)

No contact whatsoever, then, with death was permissible for the High Priest: that is, symbolically, he stood before Israel as one who was untouched by death, one exempt from its ravages.

Now the author of Hebrews knew that the One whom he had affirmed to have been free from sin in the days of his abasement and temptation, had *by now* actually ceased to stand in any relation whatsoever to death. In Jesus, in fact, not one requirement of priesthood only (as in the case of Aaron), but all three – firstly, sympathy; secondly, sinlessness (and that genuine, authentic sinlessness); and, now thirdly, immunity also to death – were all to be found united. The author had before laboured to reconcile his readers to the Cross by showing that the Son had first, as Saviour, to be lower in nature than the angels. He would now make them see as well that the relationship to death which that had entailed had in no way disqualified Jesus from priesthood, precisely because that relationship had, with his glorification, ceased utterly to be! All that in fact remained of his earthly weakness now was his *memory* of it: the weakness, as such, no longer existed. Jesus thus had all the capacity for sympathy which Aaron had had, yet he possessed in addition two advantages, from possession of which Aaron, as a sinner, had been debarred – firstly a sinlessness which permitted him to plead with power before God for the sins of his people and, secondly, an endlessness of life which spelt salvation for those who were thus forgiven. That is, all that Aaron had been able to offer to the Israelites in symbol – but in symbol only – Jesus could now offer to Christians, in reality. By identification with him as their representative, other men could now, in their turn, be regarded by God as likewise without sin and exempt from death. It was for that very reason, indeed, that God had appointed Christ as Priest, as well as marked him out as the supreme sacrifice for sin. It was essential, in fact, for men's salvation that he who had made expiation for their sin should also be the one to intercede for them before God, and thus in his own person bring them to God.

## Sacrifice first – intercession second

Now this significant order of events – Sacrifice first, Priestly intercession second – would need no explanation, or even assertion, for the readers. To them it would be familiar and natural. Thus when the time came for the writer to cite his positive proof that Jesus had in turn been appointed high Priest (and so by implication had replaced the Aaronic priesthood by his own) he simply took that order of events for granted. But, unless we today realize this, the actual form which he gave to his proof will appear a little quaint to us. That form was as follows. Having first stated, "Now no man taketh this honour unto himself but he that is called of God, as was Aaron", the author thereupon added:

> "So also Christ glorified not himself to be made an high priest, but he that said unto him, Thou art my Son, today have I begotten thee. As he saith also, in another place, Thou art a priest for ever after the order of Melchisedec." (Hebrews 5:4-6)

If we forget what was the writer's preoccupation at the time we shall miss the point of the first of these two quotations. The fact was that, for the author, the antitypical High Priest prefigured in the person of Aaron was One who had *at first* been (like Aaron) "compassed about with infirmity", but who had also *thereafter* (unlike Aaron) attained to immunity from such infirmity. That is, he was intent on showing to his readers that God's work in Christ was one and indivisible, even though it embraced two phases of

## "CROWNED WITH GLORY AND HONOUR"

experience by Christ himself. He wished the life of Christ in the flesh – culminating in the death of the Cross – and the new life of Christ in the spirit – the glorious outcome of that death – to be seen as stages in one and the same process of salvation with the Cross as the nexus between them.

What places this fact beyond doubt is his commentary on these Old Testament verses. There the significance of both Scriptures is expounded in strict historical sequence. It is firstly with Jesus "in the days of his flesh", secondly with Jesus having been "made perfect", that the writer is concerned – true to his aim everywhere in the letter of reconciling the glory of Christ with the humiliation and the shame that had gone before it. Thus, "Thou art my Son, today have I begotten thee" pointed to the first birth – that is, the physical, the human birth – of the Son: for it was with that birth that "the days of his flesh" had begun, those days when, having "offered up prayers and supplications with strong crying and tears unto him that was able to save him from death", he "was heard in that he feared" – those days during which, "though he were a Son" (as Psalm 2:7 served to show) he had yet "learned obedience by the things which he suffered" (5:7,8).

### Made perfect

But to those days, during which Jesus knew human infirmity experimentally, there had been a glorious sequel. The Son had since – and moreover (as had earlier been shown) in direct consequence of his obedience – undergone a second birth – that is, been the subject of a change of nature, or, to quote the writer himself, had been "made perfect" So, at once the second Old Testament scripture became valid:

"*Being made perfect*, he became the author of *eternal* salvation unto all them that obey him; called of God an high priest *after the order of Melchisedec.*" (5:9,10)

Have we rightly construed the phrase "made perfect"? Certain expositors, overlooking the context and failing to observe the thought sequence here, would restrict its meaning, and interpret it as stating only that Jesus was completely suited – fully consecrated – to the task of priesthood allotted him. With that particular meaning we cannot indeed quarrel; but there is undoubtedly a reference also to another factor, one which was indispensable to this fitness of Christ for priestly office – i.e., to his ascent to spirit nature. Behind the words here lies the idea of Christ attaining to glory and ascendancy over the angels, after having first been born lower than they, and thereby been a partaker absolutely of flesh and blood. The fact is that attainment would not have been possible without the Resurrection and the change of nature consequent upon it. As had been stated earlier, it had been the Father's express purpose to make the Son *"perfect* through sufferings".

It was this consideration which alone could make those sufferings acceptable to the readers, as the writer knew only too well. Thus his aim throughout was to show the exalted Jesus whom he preached, and the suffering Jesus of whom his readers were now becoming ashamed, to be one and the same person – One who had proved that "through death" he had "destroyed him that had the power of death" by himself rising from the dead to life unending. While the verb translated "make perfect", used repeatedly in this epistle, has undoubtedly at times the restricted meaning of "consecrate" (e.g., 9:9; 10:1,14), it makes equally obvious reference at others to an attainment to the eternal realm which lies beyond this earthly life. Thus the Old Testament worthies "received not the promise", in hope of which they lived and died, because God has "provided some better thing for us, that they without us should not be *made perfect*" (11:40). Similarly the heavenly Jerusalem – i.e., the immovable Kingdom of the Christian – is defined as the abode of "the spirits of just men made perfect" (12:23). It is interesting therefore to find the writer, in quite another context, declaring that if Jesus "were *on earth*, he should *not* be a priest, seeing there are priests (i.e., on earth) that offer gifts according to the law"

(8:4). Language such as this would not have been used unless, by now, he were taking it for granted that Jesus could not have been called to priesthood before he had attained to spirit nature.

## Within the veil

Actually at 5:10 the author abruptly broke off his comments on priesthood to rebuke his readers for their spiritual dullness, and to warn them sternly against all thought of apostasy (pp. 62,63), but skilfully he brought them back to the point of departure and so to the great theme of Christ's priesthood. He did so, we note, in accordance with his original assertion – as interpreted by us – that Jesus, "being made perfect", was "called of God an high priest after the order of Melchisedec" (5:9,10). First he defined the Christian hope as one which "entereth into that within the veil", knowing that his readers would – as always, being zealous Jews – grasp the import of his language, and see it to mean that Jesus had attained to the realm of spirit existence. Then next he pointed out that because Jesus had done this, so also could they. "Within the veil", said he, "the *forerunner* is for us entered, even Jesus". But in what sense had Jesus entered 'for us'? In that he had been "made a priest for ever after the order of Melchisedec" (6:19,20). And, with that assertion, the author was once more completely back on his subject. So we, like his readers, plunge with him now into that Christological study of Melchisedec, for which they, due to their own neglect, were so unprepared.

## Eternal priesthood

The importance which he attached throughout this study to the fact that Christ was an *undying* Priest is remarkable. We could indeed want no clearer proof of the correctness of the sense which we have attached to the expression "made perfect" in 5:9, and with that notion uppermost in our minds, as it was in the author's, we shall not fail to understand aright his reasoning in this section of the epistle. It was with the contrast between Christ the undying, and priests who are "men that die" (7:8) that he was alone ultimately concerned.

By his own terms of reference he was, of course, precluded from regarding Melchizedek as being anything but a man – every high priest is "taken from among men" and "ordained for men". He would therefore assume that his readers realized that Melchizedek had been born in the normal way, and had in due course died. That, however, did not prevent him – given his avowed intention of construing the story of Melchizedek Christologically (5:11,12) – from declaring Melchizedek to have been "without father, without mother, without descent (i.e., priestly pedigree), having neither beginning of days, nor end of life". For, knowing Jesus to have been "called of God an high priest for ever after the order of Melchisedec", and knowing that Jesus had therefore superseded Melchizedek, no less than Aaron, as priest, he felt justified in seeing in Melchizedek, in the same way as in Aaron, a type of Christ. Now in Scripture were to be found the fullest details concerning both the parentage and the decease of Aaron. But not so with Melchizedek: since the priesthood of Jesus was one pertaining to the eternal realm, it was only to be expected that such physical details would be altogether absent from the Old Testament record of this priest who appeared there solely and exclusively to prefigure Jesus. In Scripture, in fact, Melchizedek was essentially intended to serve as a symbolic son of God become priest. As such he did not (in the record that is) either begin his function as priest on account of some qualification of birth, or relinquish it on account of death. As the writer expressed it:

"This Melchisedec ... abideth a priest continually."
(7:1-3)

Before this man, therefore, seeing that he was, so to speak, the Son of God in person, the Aaronic priesthood had perforce to make obeisance. In the person of Abraham it had in fact done so (verses 4-10).[1] But the

---
1. We might remind ourselves in passing that nothing is more

actual – as distinct from the typical – Son of God having come, that avowal needed now to be made afresh. The contemporary priesthood could hardly be expected to make it; but it could none the less, and should, in fact, now be made, by proxy, in the person of these Jewish Christians who were showing themselves so loyal to that priesthood. And that avowal was *ipso facto* recognition that Christ had *supplanted* Aaron. For in him, all that was accomplished merely in symbol by the Aaronic priesthood had become fact. That priesthood, like the Law itself (verse 19), could never give men access to the *eternal* realm; but Christ could, for he was himself, now that he had been glorified, an actual member of that realm. So he and Aaron could not, in the nature of things, be rivals, for the all-sufficient reason that his priesthood was intrinsically superior, being altogether independent of flesh descent.

"After the similitude of Melchisedec there ariseth another priest, who is made, not after the law of a carnal commandment, but after the power of an endless life. For he testifieth, Thou art a priest *for ever* after the order of Melchisedec."   (verses 15-17)
And here, we note again, everything depends upon the fact that the Jesus who was appointed priest was the Jesus who had "the power of an endless life" – that is, the Jesus who, having first been compassed with infirmity, had thereafter been "made perfect".

**Unending exaltation**

From this point onward in the argument the writer's concerns became wider, and a number of telling observations were made by him which, being closely related to themes which require special treatment on their own account, will engage our attention later. We may therefore, in pursuance of our special interest at this stage, confine ourselves now to one of these only. The Aaronic priests, argued the writer, "were

characteristically Semitic, or more effectively stamps this epistle as one written by a Jew to Jews, than this argument based on physical descent.

many", "because they were not suffered to continue by reason of death" (7:23). How wonderful, then, was the superiority over them of Christ, as Priest, being as it was consequent upon his own deathlessness – "this man, because he continueth ever, hath an unchangeable priesthood" (verse 24).

In the face of this momentous fact could the readers hesitate any longer? Would they not be guilty of incredible folly if they chose Aaron in preference to Christ?

"Wherefore [urged the writer once again, as he had urged them earlier (5:9)] he is able also to save them to the uttermost that come unto God by him, seeing he ever liveth to make intercession for them." (7:25)

And then came the master strokes, driving home all that had been said before concerning both Aaron and Christ, and once again relating the temporary abasement of Christ to the unending exaltation which had followed it:

"Such an high priest became us, who is holy, harmless, undefiled, separate from sinners, and made higher than the heavens." (verse 26)

"Holy", and "harmless" – Christ had been this even in his weakness. "Undefiled" – this was also true of him morally during us time of abasement, but that his full participation in "flesh and blood" should not prove a stumbling-block any further to the readers, the word was here given its absolute meaning, for with his exaltation, as has been repeatedly stated, all physical contact with sin and with death ceased utterly. He became "separate from sinners" finally and absolutely, having now been made "higher than the heavens". Aaron had in *symbol* also been all these things: but how his symbolic perfection would pale before the great reality to which these highly significant words referred! For the fact was that "the law maketh men high priests which have infirmity". But not so the promise made in Psalm 110:4, which, like that made in verse 1, envisaged none but Jesus and him exalted above all infirmity. That is, in contrast to the Law, "the word of the oath, which was since the law, maketh the Son (High Priest) who is *perfected for evermore*" (7:28, RV). Here, then, not in terms of sympathy only, but in terms also of power, was "a *great* High Priest" indeed!

# 7

## "ONE SACRIFICE FOR SINS FOR EVER"
*The all-sufficiency of salvation through Christ.*

THE writer of Hebrews could neither too often, nor too forcefully, bring home to his readers what, for want of a better word, we might term the 'onceness' of God's work in Christ.

The keynote was struck at the outset. Many, he declared, had been the times, diverse the forms of revelation employed, and numerous the prophets of whom use had been made, when God had spoken in the past to the fathers. But how different had been His speaking of late in Christ. This had been done not in many but in one, and him a Son – proof in itself that the revelation so made had been not only complete, but final – and thus, of necessity, *unrepeatable* (1:1,2).

Yet as the prophets had been many, so had the priests. Aaron had been obliged to make way for Eleazar, Eleazar for Phinehas, Phinehas for another, and likewise every other priest down through the ages. "They truly were many priests, because they were not suffered to continue by reason of death." But how different, again, was the situation in the case of the Son – "This man, because he continueth ever, hath an unchangeable priesthood" (7:23,24). Once more the function of many had been fulfilled in One. They, therefore, in their multiplicity, had of necessity been superseded by him in his uniqueness, so that their services as priests could now be lawfully dispensed with as outmoded.

But that being so, the question at once presented itself to the readers – 'How precisely do we stand, then, in relation to those sacrifices which it has always constituted the daily duty of these priests to offer?' To answer that question, the author, true to his method, would refer them, not only as usual to the testimony of the Law in general, but more especially this time to the lessons taught by the ritual of the Day of Atonement in particular.

### The 'once-ness' of Christ's work

He had, in fact, given early notice of this latter intention. This was not immediately obvious in his first mention of Jesus as a High Priest, since at that stage he was primarily concerned with stressing the Son's abiding sympathy with his suffering human brethren (2:17,18). But in his next mention he had gone a vital step further, declaring "that we have a great high priest that is *passed into the heavens*" (4:14). The allusiveness of that language would not be lost on these readers; but, as we have seen, its import was made plainer still when the author proceeded next to define "the hope set before us" as one "which entereth into that *within the veil*", and then to prove the fact by demonstrating that Christ's priesthood was of necessity a priesthood "for ever" (6:18-20). Thus the crucial factor for both writer and readers was the *sphere* of Christ's ministry as Priest: he had gone whither no Aaronic priest had ever gone – into heaven itself. "For such an high priest became us," said he, "who is made *higher than the heavens*". He would now, therefore, on that basis, proceed to demonstrate to his readers that, as Christians, theirs was a High Priest "who needeth not daily, as those high priests, to offer up sacrifice, first for his own sins, and then for the people's: for this he did *once* when he offered up himself" (7:26,27). That is, as earlier (in terms of Psalm 8), he had reconciled and related the exaltation of the Son to his prior humiliation and suffering, so now (in terms of the ritual of the Day of Atonement) would he reveal the essential 'once-ness' of Christ's work as Priest on the one hand and as sacrifice on the other. So doing he would more than demonstrate the futility of continued animal sacrifices.

He from the outset could, of course, see what had obviously not yet struck his readers – that in one significant respect the Day of Atonement adequately demonstrated that futility anyway. For the key to the importance of that Day was the author's own criterion of 'once-ness'. It operated thus: daily throughout the year which had gone before, offering after offering had been made upon the sacred altar, each in its special way making atonement for the offerer's sins, but on this momentous day all these offerings were treated as though they had never in fact been made!

"On that day [said God] shall the priest make an atonement for you, to cleanse you, that ye may be clean from all your sins before the LORD. It shall be a sabbath of rest unto you, and ye shall afflict your souls, by a statute for ever ... and this shall be an everlasting statute unto you, to make an atonement for the children of Israel for all their sins once a year." (Leviticus 16:30-34)

"Atonement for *all* their sins", said the Law; and that "*once* a year". There was no mistaking the import of those words: here was finality, but it was finality, we note, achieved at *the expense of* the multiplicity of sacrifices so punctiliously offered during the whole year just gone by. It was no use anyone therefore pleading exemption from the stern provisions of the Law, on the score that some special offering which he had made had cleansed him utterly from sin. The Law was inflexible:

"It is a day of atonement to make an atonement for you before the LORD your God. For whatsoever soul it be that shall not be afflicted on that same day, he shall be cut off from among his people. And whatsoever soul it be that doeth any work in that same day, the same soul will I destroy from among his people." (23:28-30)

Thus were all called upon to recognize that their offerings, however numerous and however sincerely offered, had in fact been devoid of atoning power. So in its own special way the Day of Atonement, precisely because of what it was – a unique day in the year – stood as a witness to the futility of repeated sacrifice.

Yet, for all this, its 'once-ness' was more apparent than real, and the very witness which it bore to the futility of all previous sacrificial ritual, it bore no less certainly to the futility of its own. For while the benefits of its special offerings extended back over the year which had just gone by, no mention whatsoever was made of the year which lay immediately ahead, let alone of the succession of years extending further still into the future. Twelve months later, the whole solemn, awe-inspiring process of atonement had to be gone through anew. The plain fact was that as prophet had had to make way for prophet, and priest for priest, so had one Day of Atonement to give place inexorably to the next – year in year out, generation after generation, with never an end to the sequence. Far, therefore, from witnessing to its ability to secure for men an effectual and abiding atonement for their sins, the Law, by the repetitiveness of this ritual, rather confessed its essential inability to do so.

This, in due course, the writer would not fail to point out, arguing that if effectual, the offerings would have "ceased to be offered", and that by them there was only *"remembrance* again made of sins every year" (Hebrews 10:1-3).

### Contrasting priesthoods – Aaron and Christ

But before he would – or, in fact, could – so boldly write off the ritual of the Day of Atonement as valueless in itself, the writer would first use it as an object lesson, and demonstrate that it had nevertheless had a value – that of bearing prophetic witness to the certainty of an eventual *all-availing* expiation for men's sins – and so to the possibility for sinful man of direct access to the actual presence of God most holy.

Now for this purpose a parallel, as well as a contrast, had to be drawn between the work of Aaron and that of Christ, as Priests. This of necessity (as had been already hinted) presupposed a parallel to exist between their respective spheres of operation as Priests. But this, in turn, witnessed to the existence of a parallel between the sacrifice made by each, as a prior condition of entry "into that within the veil". Sacrifice and priesthood were, in fact, indissolubly linked. What rendered sacrifice so pre-eminent, however, in the case of Christ was the essential nature of his priesthood. So upon that the writer took care to place special emphasis at the very commencement of his argument.

"Now of the things which we have spoken [said he] this is the sum [or, *essence*]: We have such an high priest who is set on the right hand of the throne of the Majesty *in the heavens*." (8:1)

"In the heavens": that is where the stress fell. That is what justified the writer in immediately declaring Jesus to be "a minister of the sanctuary and of the true tabernacle (i.e., the actual abode of God) which the Lord pitched and not man" (verse 2). But apart from his work as the presenter of gifts and sacrifices the role of the earthly priest had no meaning; no more then, argued the writer, had that of the heavenly priest either.

"For every high priest is ordained to offer gifts and sacrifices: wherefore it is of necessity that this man (i.e., Jesus) have somewhat also to offer." (verse 3)

And to offer, of course, *in heaven* – as the following comment served to make clear:

"For [argued the writer] if he were *on earth*, he should *not be a priest*, seeing that there are priests that offer gifts according to the law." (verse 4)

But Christ, of course, was not on earth; he, therefore, had not assumed priesthood to offer such gifts as these, but a greater offering of which these were – like the priests who presented them – a mere ritual example and shadow (verse 5). As the writer expressed it – "But now" (i.e., now that Christ – as he had so carefully stressed – was in heaven itself), "But now hath he obtained a more excellent ministry" (verse 6).

## Ministries in heaven and on earth

And here, before we plunge with the writer into his later exposition, we must pause, and take conscious note of the fact (otherwise we shall not understand that exposition aright but shall misconstrue his terms) that to this more excellent ministry in heaven the only possible earthly counterpart was the ministry of the Aaronic priest in *the Most Holy Place on the Day of Atonement*. Upon that alone did the writer have his eye. Matters such as Aaron's prior washing his body, or subsequent conduct of the ritual of the scapegoat, had therefore no direct bearing on his argument (Leviticus 16:4,20-28). His sole concern, for the moment, was with the uniqueness of the Day of Atonement – and its symbolic importance on that account – as the one and only day in each year when entry was made *beyond the veil* separating the Most Holy from the Holy Place. Of the ordinary (that is, the normal, daily) activity of the Aaronic priests, he could, in his treatment of the type, take no cognizance whatever: because it stopped short at the veil, and because it could proceed no further, that service could not possibly for him prefigure the work of the One appointed priest "for ever" and to minister "in heaven". Only the extraordinary (that is, the abnormal, annual) activity of the High Priest could accomplish that particular purpose.

But so doing, that activity, argued the writer, proved the imperative necessity of sacrifice as a condition of Christ's entry into heaven. "Now when these things were thus ordained", said he, commenting on the arrangement of the Tabernacle, "the priests went always into the first tabernacle, accomplishing the service of God" (Hebrews 9:6). Not a mention here of blood we note. There could have been, since sometimes blood was in fact taken into the Holy Place to be smeared on the horns of the Incense Altar (e.g., Leviticus 4:7,18). But this was the exception, not the rule. Access was not dependent directly upon sacrifice, and was possible daily and by many priests. Quite otherwise, however, was the situation with regard to the Most Holy:

"Into the second went the high priest alone once every year, not without blood, which he offered for himself, and for the errors of the people."

(Hebrews 9:7)

The writer would have his readers remember, then, that one priest only was granted this privilege, and that on one signal occasion only in each year, yet always upon the indispensable condition of taking with him sacrificial *blood*.

## The Law's powerlessness

This entry of the High Priest *alone* – that is to the exclusion of the Aaronic Priesthood as an institution – was thus highly suggestive, argued the writer. Thereby the Holy Spirit was "this signifying, that the way into the holiest of all was not yet made manifest, while as the first tabernacle was yet standing" (verse 8). "The first tabernacle" here in question was the Holy Place, as he himself had just indicated twice (verses 2,6). So long as that, said he, was the appointed means of approach to God, no access to the true presence of God was in fact possible. Each day throughout the year the priesthood had to await a special day, and an exceptional arrangement, in order for penetration into "the holiest of all" to be achieved, Thus the Holy Place served only as "a figure for the time then present" – it was emblematic that is, of the era of the Law's period of applicability and so of the Law's powerlessness to bring men to God. It stood for that age "in which were offered both gifts and sacrifices that could not make him that did the service perfect, as pertaining to the conscience". A man might conform scrupulously to the Law eating only clean meat (Leviticus 11), drinking only ceremonially unpolluted water or wine (verse 32; Numbers 19:15), washing his body whenever the Law prescribed, and punctiliously avoiding physical contact with ceremonial uncleanness in every form – but he was not a whit the better spiritually or morally on that account. All these ritual ordinances were therefore imposed on men only until the time of reformation prefigured by the High Priest's entry into the Most Holy Place (Hebrews 9:9,10).

By its repetitiveness, however, even that annual entry proved itself to belong only to the time of waiting, and not in fact to constitute the time of reformation.

"But Christ [said the author, making triumphant appeal to the nature of Christ's priesthood, which he had so carefully underlined at the outset] being come an high priest of good things to come, by a greater and more perfect tabernacle, not made with hands, that is to say, not of this building; neither by the blood of goats and calves, but by his own blood he entered in once *into the holy place*, having obtained eternal redemption." (verses 11,12)

Here was reality at last: entry had been effected into the true Holy Place – that is, into heaven itself. Upon that fact the argument in favour of continued animal sacrifice ultimately foundered – a truth which the writer here summarily expressed by saying that the entry into the holy place was simultaneously the obtaining of an "*eternal* redemption". In the type, the ministry of the priest in the Most Holy had been temporary only, which made it obvious that the atonement there made had been temporary also. But Jesus' entry – precisely because it was an entry into the *eternal* realm – was not temporary and could not be temporary: it was for all time, since his change of nature (of which the entry was the token) was an unrepeatable, irreversible, experience. That entry had, therefore, been made "once" – once and for all, that is. So, said the author (arguing back to the sacrifice of himself previously made by Jesus in order to procure the blood without which he could not have entered), Jesus had, on entering, obtained not a temporary, but an *eternal*, redemption.

## Death of sacrifice outside the tabernacle

But (it might be rejoined) was not that redemption obtained simultaneously with the Sacrifice rather than with the Entry? Proleptically, yes: actually, no. And proof of the fact lies in the Law itself.

Sacrifice – since to be sacrifice it entailed the *death* of the victim offered – was always conducted outside the Tabernacle. Never did it take place within the Tabernacle, least of all within the veil. Yet – and this point is vital – never did sacrificial death suffice in itself to obtain the redemption of sins. The infliction of that death was always the work of the one who presented the offering. Therefore, since by the laying on of hands that offering had become a symbol of himself (Leviticus 4:4), when the offerer put it to death he in symbol put himself to death. But from that moment onwards priestly intervention became imperative, for not until the blood surrendered in death by his offering had been brought into contact with the altar did that death acquire atoning value. On this matter the Law was categorical:

"For [said God] the life of the flesh is in the blood: and I have given it to you *upon the altar* to make an atonement for your souls."  (17:11)

Such was the fundamental law, governing all normal cases. Variations of it, we observe, far from modifying its significance, served rather to heighten it. Such a variation occurred in the case of the special Sin Offerings made occasionally for a priest or the whole nation (4:1-22). In this case the taking of some of the blood into the Holy Place was an essential first step in procuring the atonement sought. But – and this was the point fundamental to the author's argument – in the unique case of the bullock and the goat offered in sacrifice on the Day of Atonement, no expiation of sin could possibly be effected unless, and until, their blood was brought *actually within the veil*. Their blood was in fact shed specifically for that purpose; so that, properly speaking, even though the animals themselves were sacrificed outside the veil, it was *inside* the veil alone that atonement was actually made. It was on that basis therefore that the author, having previously so carefully underlined the fact that, as Priest in the *heavenly* realm, Jesus was a Priest for *ever*, now argued that Jesus had by his entry with the blood provided by his prior sacrifice effected a redemption which was likewise "for ever".

**Christ, both Offering and Priest**

Thus does the Law help us to relate correctly the Sacrifice and the Entry. But so doing it complicates for us the task of relating the Sacrifice and the Priesthood; for in the ritual of the Day of Atonement not only was the one who offered the Sacrifice also the one who made the Entry, but he was, at both stages of the ritual, a Priest! So the question naturally arises, Did Christ serve as both Victim *and Priest* when he "offered himself"? That is, was he after all a Priest *before* his death, because unless he were a Priest he could not make of himself a sacrifice?

The normal ritual of sacrifice surely provides us with the solution to this problem. Since the unique feature of the ritual of the Day of Atonement was the entry into the Most Holy Place, that entry had perforce to be made by one who was priest. For this reason in his discussion of the ritual, the writer of Hebrews as naturally used the term, "High Priest", as he did expressions such as "blood", "holy place" and so on. But the testimony of the standard ritual remained explicit – priestly presentation of atoning blood commenced not before, but directly after the offerer's sacrificial slaughter of his offering (that is, the offerer's ritual offering of himself). The offering "of himself" by Jesus on the Cross did not therefore constitute an act intrinsically priestly. And in that connection it can hardly be without significance that the Law required the High Priest who officiated to do so in a simple white robe which was duly exchanged for his normal vestments – but not, in actual fact, until the blood of the bullock and of the goat offered for himself and the people had been duly presented to God within the veil, and the scapegoat had subsequently been released in token of the fact that atonement had thereby been effected (Leviticus 16:4,23,24).

At all events, of this much we can be certain – that Jesus presented himself as an offering to God in *two* senses, not one – the first "on earth", the second "in heaven", and that for the writer to the Hebrews his unique work as Priest belonged to the second stage of presentation. It was because Christ's Entry into heaven had the essential quality of 'once-ness' that the author attributed that same quality to his prior Sacrifice. And not vice-versa: once again it was the glory which gave meaning to the sufferings, though the two being inseparable the fact remained that the glory would not have been possible without the sufferings – as would emerge more clearly in the course of the argument to follow.

## The sacrifice of Christ and animals contrasted

For the moment, however, the author was concerned only to heighten the contrast between the typical and the anti-typical. To do so he reminded his readers of the "carnal" nature of purification effected by animal sacrifice – even that effected on the Day of Atonement. Ostensibly this latter was for "sins", but in the Law those "transgressions" were indistinguishable from the "uncleanness" which was so powerful a symbol of them. Thus when confessing over the head of the scapegoat "the iniquities, the transgressions and the sins" of the people, the Priest of necessity referred to ceremonial as much as to moral, defilement (verses 16,21). In reality the blood of the bullock and the goat – they being non-moral unconsenting creatures – availed only to cancel that particular defilement, in the same way as the ashes of the Red Heifer – another non-moral unconsenting creature – imparted to water the power to purify a man of a purely *bodily* condition ascribed to him on account of *bodily* contact with death, without there being any express mention made in the ritual of his actual moral and spiritual condition. This latter condition was simply assumed to be one of "dead works", and thus to be depicted in the ceremonially "dead" condition of his body. But not professing to purge his *conscience* from those same "dead works", or sinful acts, the "water of separation" obviously did not do so in actual fact. That is, its potency stopped short at the body, and operated only on this mortal side of the veil.

But not so the offering of Christ – that is, his offering of himself on the Cross. This was an offering made on the spiritual plane, by a moral being, fully consenting to his own death; an offering, moreover, made with a view to achieving access into the eternal realm, and fully capable of achieving it because of his moral spotlessness. For the blood shed in his death would partake of that same spotlessness, and thus, after death, be fit for presentation direct to God in the true "Most Holy Place". Not that it was the literal blood of Jesus which would be presented thus to God, but rather the life – now become a *resurrected* life – which (according to the principle enunciated in Leviticus 17:11) the blood served in the ritual to represent.[1] The moment, therefore, the resurrected Jesus ascended to spirit nature his sacrifice immediately acquired absolute potency – potency consequently to purge even the conscience itself. As the writer so powerfully expressed it:

"For if the blood of bulls and of goats, and the ashes of an heifer sprinkling the unclean, sanctifieth to the purifying of the flesh; how much more shall the blood of Christ, who through the eternal Spirit offered himself without spot to God, purge your conscience from dead works to serve the living God?"
(Hebrews 9:13,14)

He could bring men though "dead" (in trespasses and sins) to the "living God", because he himself, despite his death, was now again living – and that for ever. As the writer had earlier expressed it:

"This man, because he continueth ever, hath an unchangeable priesthood. Wherefore he is able also to save them to the uttermost that come unto God by him, seeing he ever liveth to make intercession for them." (7:24,25)

---

[1] The use of ritual terminology must not, be it noted, mislead us into confusing the antitype with the type.

So by his death, as would later be even more powerfully demonstrated, the New Covenant – promising utter forgiveness of sin – was ratified and became at last effective. But without his blood it could not have come into force, but would have remained an empty promise of blessing, for (as had been so signally demonstrated in the early stage) death could only be undone firstly by death, and then, and only then, by resurrection (9:15-17).

## Requisite death and resurrection

In the person of Christ – as Offering on the one hand, and Priest on the other – the requisite death and the requisite resurrection had both been accomplished: that is, he had offered himself "through the eternal spirit" (verse 14). It was that same spirit which ensured continuity, where death would normally have served as an insurmountable barrier. But as for the death itself (which he of necessity had to undergo in the course of thus offering himself), that could in no way have been circumvented: the very nature which he possessed, in order to be able to undergo it for others, demanded it of himself' *for himself*. As had earlier been shown, "by the grace of God" he was all mankind in one (2:9, cf. p. 79). Of old the sins of Israel regularly defiled the Tabernacle in *all* its parts, so that blood had to achieve atonement for those sins by purifying each of those parts in turn, (the holy sanctuary, the tabernacle of the congregation, and the altar – Leviticus 16:33; cf. 15-19). But this arrangement witnessed to the fact that sin, being a moral and spiritual phenomenon, had correspondingly defiled the very abode of God Himself; so that the One to make entry into that sanctuary had perforce, both to be sinless in himself, yet also to have first undergone sacrificial death in order to make the removal of that defilement possible. Only thus could he cleanse the men who had no right to enter with him and restore to them the privilege of free access to God which had been lost for them in Eden. So the writer argued:

"It was therefore necessary that the patterns of things in the heavens should be purified with these (i.e., blood offerings); but the heavenly things themselves with better sacrifices than these. For Christ is not entered into the holy places made with hands, which are the figures of the true; but into heaven itself, now to appear in the presence of God for us."

(Hebrews 9:23,24)

We note the same insistence again − "into heaven itself" − with all its suggestions of 'once-ness', which ruled out all possibility of a repetitive entry for Christ, which was so signal a feature of the ritual of the Day of Atonement, despite its own typical "once-ness". So the writer added pointedly that there was no possibility of repetitive Sacrifice either:

"Nor yet that he should offer himself often, as the high priest entereth into the holy place every year with blood of others; for then must he often have suffered since the foundation of the world: but now once in the end of the world hath he appeared to put away sin by the sacrifice of himself." (verses 25,26)

The "appearing" before the very face of God (verse 24) was thus matched by the previous "appearing" among men, as a man, in order to put away sin (definitively and for all time) "by the sacrifice of himself" (verse 26). Thus though those who "came unto God by him" need absolute forgiveness through him every day, without ceasing, he himself has no need, in order to obtain that forgiveness for them, to do daily, what was done each Day of Atonement by the Aaronic priests. What was secured by Aaron in the sacrifice of the bullock for his own sins (that is, right of entry to the Most Holy Place for himself first) and in the sacrifice of the goat for the people's sins (that is, right of entry thereto as their representative also) was by Jesus secured by *one* offering only − his own!

"[He] needeth not daily, as those high priests, to offer up sacrifice, first for his own sins, and then for the people's: for this he did once, when he offered up himself." (7:27)

He "put away sin" as far as he himself was concerned, when on the Cross he put off that "infirmity" which he shared in common with his brethren in whom it never failed to assert itself in actual acts of sin, but which he himself knew experimentally without ever being led by it to mar the image of God in himself. But, putting it away, he put it away once and for all. Being "made perfect" he could not undo his perfection and begin the process of redemption all over again. For, in the nature of things, there was no need to do so – that redemption being, like himself (and so like his priesthood) *eternal*. So, argued the writer:

"As it is appointed unto men once to die, but after this the judgment: so Christ was once offered (*and once only*) to bear the sins of many." (9:27,28)

These were words at once sobering and encouraging. Sobering words because they were a reminder to the readers that life, with all its opportunities, could be lived only once, and that death would therefore be followed by an inescapable judgement which would settle matters for them one way or the other, for eternity. Yet they were encouraging words, too, because they also reassured the readers that Christ, having lived his life and undergone his death, had no need to do either again. All that remained for his human brethren, still themselves imperfect, to do was therefore to await his re-emergence to view from the heavenly sanctuary (not mortal like Aaron, but immortal because no longer related to sin). For that re-emergence would work the same irreversible change in them, as he himself had undergone when God brought him again from the dead and made him perfect. "Unto them", said the writer, "that look for him shall he appear the second time *without sin*" – and thus, wonderful to tell, "unto salvation" (verse 28).

Well must he have gasped in horror, no less than in indignation, at the thought that some of his readers, ceasing to look for Jesus' coming any longer, were turning their backs on that salvation and starting back on the road which could lead them only to perdition – perdition which, in common with that same salvation, would be eternal, unchangeable, irrevocable.

# 8

## "HE TAKETH AWAY THE FIRST"
*The Law repealed and replaced.*

AS, in his masterly exposition of the sacrificial and priestly work of Jesus, the author of Hebrews established point by point the exactness of the parallel between that work and the ritual of the Law of Moses, by which his readers set such store, the fact could not fail to impress itself upon them that such a parallel could be no product of chance. And if not that, what else could it be but proof that it was the same God who had been behind the work of Jesus as behind that of Moses, and therefore that the outworking of the deeper import of the Law was in fulfilment of a purpose of which God, and not man, was the initiator? Thus was cumulative witness borne to the fact that the role of the Law had, after all, been not permanent but provisional.

We have seen how the author gave the plainest intimation of this at the very commencement of his letter. "God", said he, pointedly, "hath *in these last days* spoken unto us in a Son" (1:2). The import of those words would not be missed by such readers as these. Here was one writing to them who was persuaded that with the advent of Jesus an entire epoch had come to its predestined end. And this one hint was, at significant points in the letter, reinforced by others, of which the first came in the course of the author's first solemn words of warning. There he laid stress on the fact that the outpouring of Spirit gifts, which had led to the founding of the Church at Jerusalem, had taken place according to God's will (2:4).

The importance of this factor can be gauged by the fact that, in the course of later warning and exposition, the author took care to emphasize the part played by the Holy Spirit in the education of God's people in the past – and thus, by extension, in the present crisis also. It was (ultimately) not the Psalmist, but "the Holy Spirit", which pleaded with them, as with their fathers – "Today, if ye will hear his voice, harden not your hearts" (3:7,8).

## A New Covenant

We have seen him, similarly, affirm that in the significant ritual of the Tabernacle service it was "the Holy Spirit" which was witnessing to the fact that "the way into the holiest of all was not yet made manifest", so long as that ritual continued in operation (9:8). And we shall, yet again, find him attributing to "the Holy Spirit" the great disclosure made through Jeremiah of the ultimate making of a new Covenant (10:15-17).

Now this disclosure was, for the author, of capital importance. For, however successfully he conveyed the impression that with the coming of Christ there had occurred a change which, instead of resisting, his readers ought rather to welcome with joy (because it was a change in harmony with the will of God from the beginning), the impression alone was not enough. Without explicit proof his case would have been inferential only, and thus, in the last analysis, inconclusive. But Jeremiah's prophecy provided just the proof which both he and his readers needed.

First came the plainest possible forecast of an eventual change of dispensation:

"Behold, the days come, saith the Lord, when I will make a *new covenant* with the house of Israel and the house of Judah ..." (Hebrews 8:8)

Next came a pointed setting off of the New against the Old:

"... not according to the covenant that I made with their fathers in the day when I took them by the hand to lead them out of the land of Egypt ..."

And the reason for the change was given, too:

"... because they continued not in my covenant, and I regarded them not, saith the Lord." (verse 9)

The readers would be able to appreciate just how true these last words were. They would know only too well that Israel, long before Jeremiah's day, had had to go into captivity, and that soon afterwards Judah had to undergo the same fate and for the same reason – failure to honour the Covenant made at Sinai. That is, after whole centuries of trial, the Law had proved its excellence to be solely in its power to *condemn*. What hope therefore was there left for the people? Seemingly none – that is, if this particular covenant remained in force. The situation could, however, be transformed, if in its place another were instituted, with the power to annul the condemnation in which this first Covenant had so completely involved them. And to announce the institution of just such a Covenant was Jeremiah's happy lot:

"For this is the covenant that I will make with the house of Israel after those days, saith the Lord; I will put my laws into their mind, and write them in their hearts: and I will be to them a God, and they shall be to me a people: and they shall not teach every man his neighbour, and every man his brother, saying, Know the Lord: for all shall know me, from the least to the greatest. For I will be merciful to their unrighteousness, and their sins and their iniquities will I remember no more." (Hebrews 8:10-12)

Now as this promise was so very explicit we may well wonder why in his earlier comments on Melchizedek, the author went to such trouble to establish this same fact (that the Law was destined to pass away and be superseded) *by means of inference only*. Better would it have been, it would seem at first sight to us, if he had invoked Jeremiah 31:31-34 straight away! But having acquired such respect for his debating skill, we can be sure that there was a sound reason for his seeming rashness. Let us, then, endeavour to find it.

## From priesthood to covenant

For him, as for his readers, the Levitical priesthood occupied a position of central importance in the administration of the Law. This, of course, as he well knew, was by the decree of the Law itself; so that by his assertion that it was under that priesthood that the people received the Law we must not understand him to mean that the Law itself was imposed upon the people by the priesthood. What then did he mean to affirm thereby? Simply the utter dependence of the people upon the ministrations of the priesthood – a dependence which every single enactment governing their worship and daily life alike, and chief of all the laws governing the Day of Atonement, served to illustrate. Now it was precisely this dependence which his readers were seeking to use as a reason for remaining loyal to that same priesthood! The author was thus merely using their *own* insistence that it was under that priesthood that they received the Law as a weapon *against* them. For Psalm 110:4 appointed "another" as Priest – one who should "rise after the order of Melchisedec and not be called after the order of Aaron". But Priesthood and Law being so interdependent, what could this new appointment mean (seeing that it disregarded utterly the appointment of the Law itself) but the annulment of both the appointment and the Law which made it? "For", said he, "the priesthood being changed, there is made of necessity a change also of the law" (7:11,12). The new appointment was intended, in fact, to effect what the Law – as symbolised in its priesthood – could never itself effect – the "perfection" of the people. Thus, he argued, "there is verily (i.e., in Psalm 110:4) a disannulling of the commandment going before for the weakness and unprofitableness thereof" (7:18), and "a bringing in thereupon of a better hope, through which we draw nigh unto God" (verse 19, RV). Thus this "disannulling" on the one hand was simultaneously the "bringing in of a better hope" on the other.

But what, in fact, was the better hope? – that given in Jeremiah 31:31-34, of course. So, to prepare the way for the quotation of that crucial Scripture, the author at once laid bare the import of the oath accompanying Christ's appointment to priesthood:

> "Inasmuch as not without an oath he was made priest ... by so much was Jesus made a surety of a *better covenant*." (Hebrews 7:20-22)

And in that significant transition from Priesthood to Covenant we finally locate the key to the author's whole purpose. What he was anxious that his readers should realize was that, between the assumption of priesthood by Christ and the entry into force of the New Covenant, *there was an indissoluble connection*. For plain and far-reaching though the terms were both of the psalm, and of Jeremiah's message, for long ages they each remained an unfulfilled prophecy.

How, then, did they at last become transformed from promise into *reality*? Clearly through one and the same act, that which made the New Covenant valid as a Covenant, and which, simultaneously, severing Christ's relationship to mortality, allowed "the word of the oath" to come into effect as well – in a word, through the Cross. It was the Cross which supplied the blood at once to ratify the Covenant as a Covenant (and so to effect the forgiveness of sins which it promised), and to give the resurrected Jesus the right of access into the holiest of all – the appointed sphere of his priesthood. Thus it was not with a view to convincing his readers first with tortuous argument that the author waited so long before calling Jeremiah 31:31-34 as witness to the truth of his case. His aim was rather to be able all the more convincingly to present the Cross as indispensable to the fulfilment of God's purpose as it was revealed both in explicit prophecy, and in the enigmatic testimony of the Law itself. Thus no sooner had he demonstrated the power of the blood of Christ to purge the conscience from dead works (Hebrews 9:14) than he went on to add:

> "And for this cause he is the mediator of the new testament, that by means of death, for the redemption of the transgressions that were under the first testament, they which are called might receive the promise of eternal inheritance." (verse 15)

## A better covenant

Christ was thus the mediator of the New Covenant, as Moses had been of the Old. But he was more – he was also the Covenant Victim, and as such the representative of all human parties to that Covenant – and so the maker of the Covenant in the human side. *His* death was thus in the sight of God (whose holiness had been offended by their sins) tantamount to *their* death. As such it procured for them forgiveness of their sins – sins ironically enough, that were transgressions against that very Covenant which in conformity with the promise made through Jeremiah, he had come to supersede. Apart from death, this Covenant, like the first, could not have come "of force" (7:16,17) but, on the other hand, it would have availed nothing if the death in question had been the death of any one of *them*. Jesus alone had the necessary sinlessness to ensure resumption of life after having thus first surrendered life in death – Jesus alone had the power, that is, to assume the office of Priest, as well as to serve as surety of this better Covenant (7:20-22).

No sacrifice offered under the Law had this same power. It had not even the power to effect true expiation for sin – the repetitiveness of the ritual being witness:

> "For the law having a shadow of good things to come, and not the very image of the things, can never with those sacrifices which they offered year by year continually make the comers thereunto perfect. For then would they not have ceased to be offered? because that the worshippers once purged should have had no more conscience of sins." (10:1,2)

"But", he added pointedly, "in those sacrifices there is a remembrance again made of sins every year" (verse 3). How striking a contrast between the Old Covenant, therefore, and the New which promised that there should be "*no more* remembrance" made of sins. And not that only: it also stood to reason that the continued offering of the sacrifices of the Old, after the entry into force of the New, amounted to a setting of the Old in direct opposition to the New. The readers were clearly under the impression that both could operate simultaneously. But they were sadly mistaken, being under the illusion that some positive good could be gained by continuing to present animal sacrifice, whereas in actual fact it was "*not possible* that the blood of bulls and of goats should take away sins" (verse 4). The fact that the death of Jesus took place at all was proof enough of that. But – and this was a far more important consideration for these readers – Jesus himself underwent that death in full awareness of what it was required to accomplish, and why. As the writer himself expressed it:

"Wherefore when he cometh into the world, he saith, Sacrifice and offering thou wouldest not, but a body hast thou prepared me: in burnt offerings and sacrifices for sin thou hast had no pleasure. Then said I, Lo, I come (in the volume of the book it is written of me) to do thy will, O God."   (verses 5-7)

**A body prepared**

Here in Psalm 40 was the clearest offsetting of two courses of action, of which the first was in strict conformity to the Law – the offering of sacrifice in its various forms. Language could not have been more precise, or have proved more useful to the writer at this juncture, and its testimony was that *God Himself* had dispensed with sacrifice. But he had done so in favour of an alternative procedure – the consistent and complete doing of His will in a "body prepared". That same "body" was for the writer – and could only be – the person of Jesus, since he alone perfectly performed God's will. But the suffering of death was not something distinct from the demands of that will, but rather was it the greatest demand of them all – the consummation of the obedience shown in the whole of the life which it terminated. Yet, since it was also the means appointed for the ratification of the New Covenant, which was designed to annul the very sins which the Old Covenant perpetuated, clearer proof could not be advanced that the entry into force of the New, far from being a supplementing of the Old, was a formal cancellation of it.

"Above when he said, Sacrifice and offering and burnt offerings and offering for sin thou wouldest not, neither hadst pleasure therein; which [added the writer pointedly] *are offered by the law*; then said he, Lo, I come to do thy will, O God."

To which, with crushing logic, the writer at once added:

"He taketh away the first, that he may establish the second." (10:8,9)

That is, while the first remained, the second could not come into force. Conversely, when the second came into force, the first simultaneously ceased to be valid – an event which coincided with "the death of the testator" as we have shown (9:16,17), and that according, once again, to God's express design from the commencement. "By the which *will*", then, commented the writer, "we are sanctified through the offering of the body of Jesus Christ once for all" (10:10).

## One offering

To clinch the matter he invited his readers to compare once again the work of the Aaronic priests and that of Christ in the light of the promise made to him by the Father – "Sit on my right hand, until I make thine enemies thy footstool" (1:13).

"Every priest [said he] *standeth* daily ministering and offering oftentimes the same sacrifices, which can never take away sins: but this man, after he had offered one sacrifice for sins for ever, *sat down* on the right hand of God; from henceforth expecting till his enemies be made his footstool." (10:11-13)

The bearing of this great truth on the argument in favour of the continued practice of animal sacrifice was simplicity itself to demonstrate. "By one offering", said the writer, "he hath perfected for ever them that are sanctified"; thereupon adding – and that with measured weight:

"Whereof *the Holy Spirit also* is a witness to us: for after that he had said before, This is the covenant that I will make with them after those days, saith the Lord, I will put my laws into their hearts, and in their minds will I write them; and their sins and iniquities will I remember no more."  (verses 14-17) "No more"! What point therefore could there be in seeking forgiveness in some other way seeing that it was permanently available in this way. It would amount in fact to an act of rebellion against the divine will. So there could henceforth be "no more offering" either – "Now where remission of these is, there is no more offering for sin" (verse 18). And with that the author summarily closed his case against those of his readers who were making this 'last-ditch' stand in favour of the ancient ritual of sacrifice.

## Consequences of rebellion

Many practical consequences issued from this – the greatest of them all, of course, the one embodied in his final call. But, as he expounded them one by one, he lost no opportunity of reminding them that continued adherence to the Law, in any of its forms, was essentially an act of rebellion. Their duty was plain – and that because God's intentions were made plain to them in the prophecy of Haggai (2:6,7). In Haggai's day Jeremiah's prophecies had already taken effect and the overthrow of the monarchy was an accomplished fact. But, through Haggai, God once again revealed His intention to overthrow not only the monarchy but also the whole religious order upon which Israel's life was based – that is, "not the earth only but also heaven" (Hebrews 12:26). True, beyond this work of judgement in the case of one people only, there lay also God's eventual work of judgement among and upon *all* peoples, with the ultimate overthrow of all systems of government and the establishment in their place of one universal rule redounding to His glory and to man's true well-being – "I will shake *all* nations", said God, "and the desire of all nations shall come" (Haggai 2:7). But,

## "HE TAKETH AWAY THE FIRST"

as an immediate prospect for the readers of Hebrews, there was the more urgent matter of the immediate passing away of every vestige of the Law. They were to see in this the finger of God Himself – and thus a call not to arrest it, but to reconcile themselves to it. "Let us have grace", then, urged the writer, "whereby we may serve God acceptably with reverence and godly fear". But while those timely words would suffice for the majority, he knew that a few recalcitrant spirits would still wish to defy them. So he judged it wise to cap them with the ominous reminder:

"For our God is a *consuming fire.*" (12:28,29)

# 9

## "GOD HAVING PROVIDED SOME BETTER THING"
*The need and secret of endurance.*

IT is remarkable – and therefore significant – that the author of Hebrews saw fit to administer a warning to his readers before turning to offer them words of cheer or encouragement. The implication is obvious: there was greater need for him to say, "Lest ...", than there was to say, "Let us ..." Yet his concluding call makes it equally plain that it was upon the positive note, "Let us" that he was determined eventually to end his letter. He therefore neglected no opportunity of fortifying his readers' resolution with timely words of cheer.

Not that he had smooth things to tell them. Far from it: the day of opportunity was, alas, the day also of temptation. For them, as for their ancestors, between the bondage behind, and the Land of Promise before, there lay a wilderness of trial and difficulty to be crossed. There would be much to make them question, as did their fathers, "Is the LORD among us or not?" But that would not alter the fact that God *was* in their midst, and that if in that confidence they confronted boldly each trial as it came He would be true to His promise and make them eventually partakers of His eternal Rest. God's fidelity was axiomatic: it was only theirs that was in doubt.

### Hope unto the end

Yet even that would not be in doubt if only they chose to continue as they had begun. They had shown great promise at the outset of their career as Christians, so that, despite his stern words of warning, the writer could find it possible to say:

"But, beloved, we are persuaded better things of you, and things that accompany salvation, though

"GOD HAVING PROVIDED SOME BETTER THING"

we thus speak. For God is not unrighteous to forget your work and labour of love, which ye have shewed toward his name, in that ye have ministered to the saints,[1] and do minister." (6:9,10)

But such reassuring words in no way excused them from effort. Rather was the contrary true. "We desire", said the author, "that every one of you do shew the same diligence to the full assurance of hope unto the end" (verse 11).

"Unto the end": this was already familiar language, for the author had before *argued* that only those are entitled to Rest who have accomplished their due quota of "labour" (4:10,11; cf. pp. 30-36). But he now chose to give that language a novel twist:

"We desire [besides, he added] that ye be not slothful, but followers of them who *through faith and patience* inherit the promises." (6:11,12)

## Faithful Abraham

What did he mean by this formula – "through faith *and patience*"? He would illustrate – using Abraham as example. For what were the facts? Abraham had received a whole succession of promises, each variants of the first and basic promise:

---

[1]. Some would see evidence here that the readers did not, after all, hail from Jerusalem, since its saints (i.e., Christian saints) were in constant need of assistance by Gentile Christians (1 Corinthians 16:1-3; Romans 15:25-27). But why should the necessitous saints be assumed to comprise the Christian community in Jerusalem in its entirety? Besides, Hebrews may well have been written, not to the Jerusalem church at large, but only to a special influential group within it – a group with the spiritual talent to become a company of "teachers" (this could hardly be true of all without exception in the Church) possessing also the material means to give much financial help of their own to these their needy brethren (cf. 10:34). If such be the facts it would seem logical, in view of the particular attention paid in the letter to the themes of priesthood and sacrifice, to identify that group with "the great company of priests", who, in the early days, became "obedient to the faith" (Acts 6:7). The position of such converts would by this time be more than usually complicated, as can only too easily be imagined.

"I will make of thee a great nation, and I will bless thee, and make thy name great; and thou shalt be a blessing." (Genesis 12:2)

To each of these promises in turn Abraham responded in faith; but to one in particular he had responded with pre-eminent faith – the promise that he, a man as good as dead, with a wife whose womb was now twice dead (for quite apart from her persistent sterility, she was in any case now past child-bearing age) should ultimately become the father of a multitude. When God "brought him forth abroad" and said, "Look now toward heaven, and tell the stars, if thou be able to number them: and said unto him, So shall thy seed be" (Genesis 15:5), Abraham had accepted that assurance with implicit trust: "He believed in the LORD". His reward was in one form immediate – the complete forgiveness of his sins:

"[God] counted it (i.e., his response in faith) to him for righteousness." (verse 6)

And, as a further outcome, came the birth in due course of Isaac.

But of Isaac only. In the person of this one child the promise hung upon a thread seemingly so slender that the possibility of his premature decease, before begetting a child of his own to perpetuate the line, must have been a constant anxiety to Abraham, despite his faith. And then one day came the awful order – and that an order by God Himself (by Him who had made the promise!):

"Take now thy son, thine only son Isaac, whom thou lovest ... and offer him there for a burnt offering."
(22:2)

Can we ever hope to enter fully into Abraham's feelings at that moment? We can but dimly imagine the harrowing effect of the prospect first of slaying, and then of consuming to ashes upon the fire, his own and only son – the son whose survival was the sole means whereby the promise which had given him birth could realize itself. It must have seemed so cruel a mockery, so pointless a frustration of the promise upon which so

## "GOD HAVING PROVIDED SOME BETTER THING"

much depended, that Abraham would be forced to ask himself whether the 'command' of God were not after all a delusion! But no: it was true – and the duty to obey, an inescapable one.

That sufficed for Abraham. That faith which hitherto he had been called upon to manifest only as an inward emotional response to the divine promise, he would now, because God required it of him, manifest afresh in this outward act, incompatible though it seemed with the promise itself. So, in due course, Isaac lay helpless upon the altar pyre, while his father stood over him, knife poised in hand, about to deal the fatal blow – so determined to deal it, in fact, that already, he was concerned not so much with the death of his son, as with the means whereby, despite that death, God would bring His purpose with Isaac to fulfilment.

That was enough for God. As Abraham tensed his arm to strike, an angelic voice called to him out of heaven:

"Lay not thine hand upon the lad, neither do thou any thing unto him: for now I know that thou fearest God, seeing thou hast not withheld thy son, thine only son from me." (22:11,12)

His faith had been tested to the uttermost – and he had not failed. Never would it be so tested again, nor would any contingency again arise to call in question the certain fulfilment of the promise. That promise was henceforth not *conditional* upon obedience – but *immutable* because the requisite obedience had already been shown:

"By myself have I sworn, saith the LORD, for because thou hast done this thing ... in blessing I will bless thee, and in multiplying I will multiply thy seed as the stars of the heaven, and as the sand which is upon the sea shore; and thy seed shall possess the gate of his enemies; and in thy seed shall all the nations of the earth be blessed; *because thou hast obeyed my voice.*" (verses 16-18)

## Confirmed by an oath

Before, it had been, "Abraham *believed*": here it was, "thou hast *obeyed*". There was no change in the faith which he was in each case called upon to manifest; the change lay simply in the mode of its manifestation; and what was so significant for the author of Hebrews was the fact that it was not until *after* he had thus "patiently endured" that Abraham "obtained the promise" – this last and pre-eminent promise, that is. That was why he urged his readers to be, "followers of them who through faith *and patience* inherit the promises", adding:

"For when God made promise to Abraham, because he could swear by no greater, he sware by himself, saying, Surely blessing I will bless thee, and multiplying I will multiply thee." (Hebrews 6:12-15)

But, as he here wrote, the author (unknown as yet to the readers) had in mind yet another oath – that accompanying the appointment of Christ to priestly office. So he took care at once to emphasize the significance of an oath – it is an act of "confirmation", said he, and "an end of all strife", even when it is used by men. And such, he added, is the case, too, with God in His dealings with men:

"Willing more abundantly to shew unto the heirs of promise the immutability of his counsel, [he] confirmed it by an oath: that by two immutable things, in which it was impossible for God to lie, we might have a strong consolation, who have fled for refuge to lay hold upon the hope set before us."

(6:17,18)

There followed immediately a hint that the oath of Psalm 110:4 would come in for attention later, for that hope was shown to be embodied in Jesus "made an high priest for ever after the order of Melchisedec" (verses 19,20).

And so in due course it did. The appointment of Jesus was not simply, "Thou art a priest for ever ...", but, "The Lord *sware* and *will not repent*, Thou art a priest for ever ..." (6:21). There lay the great, the

## "GOD HAVING PROVIDED SOME BETTER THING"

crucial difference between Jesus and Aaron as Priests. Both were called to office by God – but only Jesus was appointed to the accompaniment of a solemn oath and an assurance that the appointment was for all time, without qualification, and with no possibility of repeal. His position was thus akin to Abraham's – he, like the patriarch, had manifested and completed his obedience by the time the oath was sworn to him. Thereafter every thing was thereby lifted out of the realm of the contingent: God's purpose was henceforth immutable.

### Blind to the eternal

But there was so much to suggest the contrary for the readers – or so they thought; for the fault lay not with their situation but with them. They were unable to see things in eternal perspective, to look beyond the immediate and the material aspects of life. Until they could be induced to do so they could not summon the resolve to adhere to Christ in the coming crisis. But they had proved themselves quite capable of doing so in the first flush of enthusiasm for the Gospel, and all they needed to do, really, was recapture the vision which then had inspired them. So the writer pleaded:

"But call to remembrance the former days, in which, after ye were illuminated, ye endured a great fight of afflictions; partly, whilst ye were made a gazingstock both by reproaches and afflictions; and partly, whilst ye became companions of them that were so used. For ye ... took joyfully the spoiling of your goods, knowing in yourselves that ye have in heaven a better and an enduring substance."

(10:32-34)

And to reinforce his plea he brought the lesson of Abraham's example – as well as their own – to bear upon them:

"Cast not away therefore your confidence, which hath great recompence of reward. For ye have need of patience (i.e., resolution), that, after ye have done the will of God, ye might receive the promise."

(verses 35,36)

How significant by now had that expression – "the will of God" – become. It was, as previously had been so powerfully shown, the very "will" which had done away with the Old Covenant and brought the New, with its promise of eternal inheritance, into force. But it had been a will also, on that very account, which had required of Jesus obedience unto death – as earlier, in Abraham's case, it had required obedience to the very point of putting Isaac to death.

**Possible martyrdom**

The author saw, moreover – and his readers saw too – that it might be a will which required obedience unto death of them also. He therefore began at this point to orientate his argument toward the topic of martyrdom, and thus to prepare them to accept, if need be, this the extreme demand of fidelity to the Gospel.

> "We are not of them [said he inspiringly] who draw back unto perdition; but of them that believe to the saving of the soul." (10:39)

Though their bodies might die, their salvation could be certain – that was the all-important factor of which they were never to lose sight. Their faith was all the guarantee required that their longings would in the end be realized – it could make visible to them there and then the invisible reality lying behind the material order. It did for Abel, Enoch and Noah. All three had acted in the unshakeable conviction that God would eventually prove them right, even though, at the time, they themselves could not give others tangible proof of the fact. And they *were* right. But had their gaze not been directed forward they could not have endured.

Abraham had the same spiritual outlook as they – and that not only when forsaking Ur to seek the Land of Promise, but even in that Land itself. Sarah, too, had been so sustained by the conviction that God would be true to His word that she gained strength thereby to overcome the very sterility which had so long threatened to nullify His promise. Never, in fact, were any of the patriarchs daunted by the prospect of

## "GOD HAVING PROVIDED SOME BETTER THING"

having to wait for the realization of their hopes – even if it could not come till after death itself. They knew that resurrection could undo the seemingly absolute effects of death. It was only that conviction, indeed, which had enabled Abraham to demonstrate his faith in the promises by performing an act which seemed to make nonsense of them:

"He that had received the promises offered up his only begotten son, of whom it was said, That in Isaac shall thy seed be called: accounting that God was able to raise him up, even from the dead." (11:17-19)

This action in the present, with an eye to the certainties of the future, was what, similarly, had characterized Isaac when blessing Jacob and Esau concerning things to come; and, again, Jacob when blessing Ephraim and Manasseh; and Joseph, likewise, when exacting from the Israelites the pledge that, when the time came for them to depart from Egypt, his mummy should go with them.

### Example of Moses

The case of Moses was particularly apposite. He had been born at a time of persecution, but perceiving for their child a glorious destiny in God's service, Amram and Jochebed "were not afraid of the king's commandment". Heedless of the danger to themselves they preserved the life of their son. He, in due course, acted likewise, formally renouncing his rights and privileges as the son of Pharaoh's daughter, despite the prospect that his act might bring upon him the same affliction as was being endured by his persecuted brethren. Like the faithful before him he saw beyond the present: "he had respect unto the recompence of the reward ... he *endured,* as seeing him who is invisible" (verses 26,27).

When Passover was kept in strict accordance with the divine command, the people acted on the assumption, on the one hand that judgement would come, and on the other that they themselves would escape it – that is, in a spirit of confidence concerning happenings in the *future*. Had the people feared to cross the bed of the Red Sea, in case they should be engulfed by the waters halfway, they would never have left Egypt. But confident that they would reach the other side they won for themselves deliverance. The hazards of the crossing were quickly demonstrated by the fate of the pursuing Egyptians – but, meantime, the Israelites, thanks to their faith, had reached safety. It was, likewise, with a view to the certainty of Jericho's ultimate fall that the hosts of Israel compassed the walls of Jericho, as bidden, for seven days on end – just one more example of present action being motivated by certainty concerning the future. Moreover even Rahab could give the readers a lesson in that same living by faith. Examples could, in fact, be multiplied. But they all taught the same twofold lesson – that faith is conviction of the reality and certainty of the unseen, and that, as such, it inspires men and women to *endure in adversity*.

## Suffering in faith

It is most significant that the author should have ended his argument on that particular note. In an almost breathless recital he drew up an imposing catalogue of persecution, torture, maltreatment, privation, martyrdom, and finally of fugitive existence, ill-clad and harassed, in deserts, in mountains, in dens and in caves of the earth. And all for what? All in the cause of fidelity to an ideal – an ideal certain to be realized eventually, if remaining at present unfulfilled.

> "These all, having obtained a good report through faith, received not the promise: God having provided some better thing for us, that they without us should not be made perfect." (verses 39,40)

This latter thrust was masterly. It was an invitation to the readers to join the ranks of these sufferers, since the reward to be won by *all* was the same as that which had been made sure for them, as Christians, by Christ. Made sure, moreover, by that death which had made of him the greatest and most glorious sufferer of all. Inspired by these their ancestors, and especially by him, their Lord, they could be prevailed upon to shake off their spiritual sloth and apathy, and to resist the insidious propaganda which threatened to subvert them.

"Wherefore [said he, choosing every word with care and tact] seeing we also are compassed about with so great a cloud of witnesses, let us lay aside every weight, and the sin which doth so easily beset us, and let us run with patience the race that is set before us, looking unto Jesus the author and finisher of our faith; who for the joy that was set before him endured the cross, despising the shame, and is set down at the right hand of the throne of God. For consider him that endured such contradiction of sinners against himself, lest ye be wearied and faint in your minds." (12:1-3)

Cause enough there was to be wearied and faint, as he well knew. But would they be so weak as to give up *now*, when as yet the struggle against the temptation to apostasy had not even demanded death itself of them, but ostracism only? Feeble in the extreme would their faith prove to be if they should be so quickly daunted.

But why, they might well wonder, should God thus allow the good to suffer? Granted that these worthies of old had "endured" and, after them, the Lord likewise, what was in any case the purpose of all this adversity?

When the author turned to answer this very natural enquiry, we need to remember that the argument of his second chapter, and the related argument based on Christ's capacity for priestly sympathy, lay behind him. He needed, in fact, to do no more than bring to bear upon his readers (as some of the "many sons" whom God was bringing to glory), the great principle stated by him to have been wrought out in the earthly experience of *the* Son. He was made perfect through sufferings; "though he were a Son, yet learned he obedience by the things which he suffered". That principle was *Scriptural*. God Himself had laid it down, therefore: all had been according to His will. So, to answer his readers, the author simply invoked the testimony of the Book of Proverbs, rebuking them in the process for overlooking that testimony:

"Ye have forgotten the exhortation which speaketh *unto you* as unto children, My son, despise not thou the chastening of the Lord, nor faint when thou art rebuked of him; for whom the Lord loveth he chasteneth, and scourgeth every son whom he receiveth." (verses 5,6)

God, as they well knew, had said in the past, "Israel is my son, even my firstborn" (Exodus 4:22). But that truth, far from obviating the wilderness journey, had rather necessitated it. So Moses had urged the people to reconcile themselves to its rigours as a divine discipline for their good:

"Thou shalt remember all the way which the Lord thy God led thee these forty years in the wilderness, to humble thee, and to prove thee, to know what was in thine heart, whether thou wouldest keep his commandments, or no. And he humbled thee, and suffered thee to hunger, and fed thee with manna, which thou knewest not, neither did thy fathers know; that he might make thee know that man doth not live by bread only, but by every word that proceedeth out of the mouth of the Lord doth man live." (Deuteronomy 8:2,3)

And he had thereupon added:

"Thou shalt also consider in thine heart, that, as a man chasteneth his son, so the Lord thy God chasteneth thee." (verse 5)

Jesus had understood and accepted that truth with absolute submission, not losing sight of the Promised Land through undue concern with the unpleasantness of the wilderness journey, but rather allowing the light of the one to irradiate the other: "for the joy ... set before him [he] endured the cross, despising the shame."

The author thus urged the readers to do likewise – to keep in mind once again the *goal* of their lives, the divinely appointed *end* of their suffering. The matter that should have been of prime concern for them was not their physical, but their spiritual, fate. They were misunderstanding God in expecting Him to vindicate His interest in them by an act of miraculous deliverance from their difficulties. Their earthly fathers had not spared them rigorous training. So, "shall we not much rather", said he, "be in subjection unto the Father of spirits, and live?" (12:9).

"And *live*", we note. The words were all the more powerful by contrast with the awful warning he had given that to "draw back" is to end in *perdition*. Once again the choice before the readers was an eternal choice, because the purpose of God was their eternal good.

### Refined by chastening

But as sinners they could not attain to that eternal good unless they first underwent a refining process:

> "[The] fathers of our flesh ... verily for a few days chastened us after their own pleasure; but he for our profit, *that we might be partakers of his holiness*."
>
> (verse 10)

To contract out of the refining process was thus to renounce with it the end to which it was designed to bring them. And that a *worthwhile* end, as their earthly experience itself could teach them; for which of them, able in adult years to conduct his own affairs aright, regretted the parental training which had qualified him to do so?

> "No chastening [he urged] for the present seemeth to be joyous, but grievous: nevertheless afterward it yieldeth [unto them which are exercised thereby, that is] the peaceable fruit of righteousness ... Wherefore lift up the hands which hang down, and the feeble knees."
>
> (verses 11,12)

True, to interrupt the author's exhortation of encouragement at this point, there had to come once more a brief digression, warning the readers against committing such folly as that of which Esau was guilty (verses 13-17); but back he came again to his main theme, to remind them of the goal of their wanderings:

"For ye are not come [said he] unto the mount that might be touched ... but ye are come unto mount Sion, and unto the city of the living God, the heavenly Jerusalem, and to an innumerable company of angels, to the general assembly and church of the firstborn, which are written in heaven, and to God the Judge of all, and to the spirits of just men made perfect, and to Jesus the mediator of the new covenant, and to the blood of sprinkling, that speaketh better things than that of Abel." (12:18-24)

The inspiration thus offered was just what the situation of the readers demanded. Not without good reason, in fact, had the author made the words of Isaiah his own – both by way of exhortation and of encouragement. For the prophet had envisaged others traversing a weary wilderness, who were likewise discouraged, as had been their fathers, by the rigours of the way. And to these he had first offered the reassurance:

"They shall see the glory of the LORD, and the excellency of our God [and then gone on to give the counsel] ... Strengthen ye the weak hands, and confirm the feeble knees. Say to them that are of a fearful heart, Be strong, fear not: behold, your God will come with vengeance, even God with a recompence; he will come and save you."

(Isaiah 35:1-4)

What the Hebrews needed to do was appropriate those very same words to themselves and to endure tribulation in the strength of them. For by those whose eyes behold such a vision as this – who look forward to the day when "the ransomed of the LORD shall return, and come to Zion, [and] shall obtain joy and gladness, and sorrow and sighing shall flee away" – all adversity is tolerable. Only where there is no vision do the people perish.

## "GOD HAVING PROVIDED SOME BETTER THING"

The difficulties of the Hebrews stemmed from just this loss of spiritual vision. To restore it was the object of all that the writer had to say to them about Christ their Lord. If he failed to restore it, it was not for want of effort or talent on his part, but only of faith on theirs – the faith of Abraham, the faith that *saves*.

# 10

## "LET US GO FORTH THEREFORE UNTO HIM"
*The call to action and its relevance for today.*

AMONG the cherished prerogatives of the Aaronic priesthood was that of eating the flesh of animals presented in sacrifice to God in the Tabernacle court. In the case of Burnt Offering that right was, of course, exclusively God's. He, when the Priest "burnt *all* upon the altar", in symbol consumed the whole of the flesh thus placed upon His "Table" (Leviticus 1:9; cf. Malachi 1:7). In the case of Peace Offering, on the other hand, God shared His "meal" with men. He, as was seemly, was "served" first (in the burning of the fat upon the altar); but Priest and offerer also received their portions – yet always in that order, the Priest each time taking precedence over the offerer, despite the latter's claim to receive the bulk of the sacrificial flesh. Not until the officiating Priest (who received the "right shoulder") and after him the priesthood at large (to which fell the "wave breast") had been served, did the man actually presenting the offering receive his own portion of it. In the case of Sin Offering this insistence on the pre-eminence of the priesthood became absolute – at least so far as routine cases were concerned. Here again it was God who was served with His portion first, but once that had been done, the rule was, "the priest that offereth it for sin shall eat it: in the holy place shall it be eaten ... all the males among the priests shall eat thereof: it is most holy" (Leviticus 6:24-29). No partaking of it by the offerer was permitted this time: the privilege was the Priests' exclusively. Thus did they become in the fullest sense "partakers with the altar", and were marked out as a special body enjoying intimate communion with God (cf. 1 Corinthians 9:13; 10:14-20).

## Aaronic sacrifice and ritual

Yet, the fact remained, and needed somehow to be made plain in the ritual of sacrifice, that their status was symbolic not actual, their communion apparent only and not real. So whereas it conferred this privilege of eating the Sin Offering upon the priests in these routine cases, in certain other exceptional cases the Law just as deliberately withheld it from them. Whenever a priest presented a Sin Offering on his own account, or on behalf of the nation in its entirety, the carcase of the victim had to be disposed of, not by eating in the Court, but by burning – and that not on the altar but outside the Camp (Leviticus 4:1-21). The animal's blood had in these less usual cases to be brought within the Holy Place, and the stringent ruling of the Law then was that:

"No sin offering, whereof any of the blood is brought into the tabernacle of the congregation to reconcile withal in the holy place, shall be eaten: it shall be burnt in the fire." (6:30)

Here, therefore, to counterbalance the granting of a great privilege to the priesthood was a drastic and significant limitation of it. And never was that limitation more drastic or more significant than on the Day of Atonement when promise was given that one day a true and all-availing sacrifice for sin would be made, once and for all time. For on that momentous Day, also, the carcases of the victims were in like manner burnt outside the Camp, with the result that the right to partake of their flesh was again denied absolutely to the officiating Priest (16:27).

The moral of this was that, when the antitypical Sin Offering prefigured in the ritual would eventually be offered, the Aaronic priesthood would not, as an institution, be brought by it into true fellowship with God. Other aspects of the ritual of that Day revealed that the One who would effect eventual access into the Holiest of all would be a Priest after the order not of Aaron but of Melchizedek (cf. pp. 88,89). This added aspect simply went one logical step further: it disqualified the Aaronic priesthood as such from all part or lot in the benefits which that access into the Holiest would win for men.

## The ceremonial superseded

Now in their present predicament it was desperately necessary for the Hebrews to realize the far-reaching consequences of this fact. They fondly imagined, and were even inclined to argue, that they could legitimately continue to profit from the ministry of these Aaronic priests. For them (and we can understand how hallowed tradition would dispose them to think so) religion without an earthly sanctuary and ritual was no religion at all. But the fact that they had now to face was that the ceremonial which they wished to perpetuate had been done away.

> "For [said the writer] it is a good thing that the heart be established with grace; not with meats, which have not profited them that have been occupied therein." (Hebrews 13:9)

Far, therefore, from feeling bereft of religion if bereft of ritual, they should realize themselves to be possessors of an Altar which, if not visible and tangible like that at which the contemporary priesthood ministered, had the advantage over this that it gave them genuine, and not merely valueless, symbolic, fellowship with God. So, protested the author with vigour, "we *have* an altar". But an Altar, he insisted, "whereof they have no right to eat which serve the tabernacle" (verse 10). What right had he to say that? The right conferred on him by the ritual of the Law itself.

> "For [he reminded his readers pointedly] the bodies of those beasts, whose blood is brought into the sanctuary by the high priest for sin, are burned without the camp." (verse 11)

## The voice of God

This aspect of the ritual had therefore a vital significance for the readers at the present juncture. It testified to the fact that they had – and could have – no fellowship whatsoever with the established priesthood. But it did more: it also predicted why this was so, for its significance was in reality, twofold. With inspired vision the author espied an even deeper correspondence than this first to exist here between the ritual of the Law and the situation created by the Crucifixion. Earlier on he had intimated that when the Israelites begged God to spare them the terror of having Him speak to them with His own voice, they had done more than make a request which, because it was reasonable, God had chosen to grant (Exodus 20:19). The writer had done this because he knew that in the act of approving the people's request, God had also protested:

> "O that there were such an heart in them, that they would fear me, and keep all my commandments always, that it might be well with them, and with their children for ever!" (Deuteronomy 5:23-29)

Now the people's request on the one hand, and God's rejoinder on the other, had, as he knew, proved each in the light of subsequent history to have been prophetic utterances. The sad fact was that the Israelites of the wilderness wanderings, and also their children down through the ages, had alike consistently "refused him that spake" – in a deeper sense than that of preferring a prophet's voice to that of God Himself. The Crucifixion, moreover, was but the culminating act of disobedience, for never was rebellion against God more patent than in the nation's refusal to heed His speaking in Christ. The writer had therefore been able to draw an ominous lesson for his readers from this seemingly innocent request made to God at Sinai (Hebrews 12:19,25).

## Christ rejected

In like manner he would now show them how the burning outside the Camp of the bodies of beasts offered in sacrifice on the Day of Atonement was also an event with a deeper import still than that which he had already brought to their notice. It was not enough to remind them that the Crucifixion was an Offering lying altogether outside the Mosaic order of sacrifice: the fact was of equal importance that it was a gesture of rejection of Jesus on the part of those who had had him so done to death. It was the logical outcome of a prior putting of him "outside the Camp" by his own people. The taking of him to die "outside the gate" was, in its own strange way, merely the final symbolic act in a whole process of repudiation, an avowal by the people that they desired no fellowship whatsoever with him – and thus equally a fulfilment of the ritual of the Day of Atonement. Where the murderers of Jesus had put him – outside the Camp, outside Jerusalem – the centre and symbol of the national worship – there the unbelieving brethren of these Jewish Christians wished still to keep him. What possibility was there, therefore, of fellowship between the two? There was clearly none whatever. What, for the Hebrews, was the supreme sacrifice for sin, was, for those unbelieving brethren with whom they were now contemplating joining forces, still no more than a felon's death, devoid of sacrificial meaning. Such, then, had been the irony of events, that the writer could say:

"Wherefore Jesus also, that he might sanctify the people with his own blood, suffered without the gate."
(13:12)

## Without the Camp

There, if the nation at large had its way, Jesus would continue to remain – outside the Camp. How, then, could his followers any longer remain *inside* it? The plain fact was that to continue henceforth to serve the Tabernacle was automatically to sever oneself from the true Altar. Conversely, to accept the benefits which this Altar conferred upon them equally necessitated forsaking the Tabernacle. Between the Law and the Gospel there was, in fact, not only the closest correspondence, but – as the outworking of the sacred ritual proved – the greatest antagonism also. It was for the Hebrews to face the fact, and, facing it, to forsake the Camp also themselves, joining themselves to Jesus – openly, resolutely, irrevocably – taking his reproach gladly upon themselves, as Moses himself had prospectively done so long centuries before (11:26). This would at once entail forsaking Jerusalem spiritually, but in due course, it would also entail forsaking it physically, since its doom was sealed by the purposes of God. So, duly, the writer's call came, as it was bound to come – bold, authoritative, inescapable:

"Let us go forth therefore unto him without the camp, bearing his reproach. For here we have no continuing city, but seek one to come." (13:13,14)

And if the close-knit argument from ritual which had gone just before it had a special relevance for the readers, in that they themselves were once servers at the Tabernacle altar (cf. p. 122), there would correspondingly be added pointedness and comfort in the exhortation which followed immediately upon it:

"By him therefore [said the writer] let us offer *the sacrifice of praise* to God continually, that is, the fruit of our lips giving thanks to his name." (verse 15)

## Offerings in Christ

In addition, then, to possessing an Altar of greater worth than the visible altar of the Tabernacle, the Hebrews had also the privilege of offering upon it sacrifices for whose continued offering there would always be need. One such sacrifice would be the meeting of the abuse and maltreatment of their non-Christian brethren with true Christian love.

"To do good, and to communicate [said the author] forget not: for with *such* sacrifices God is well pleased." (verse 16)

And they could begin to show that love by obeying their spiritual leaders whose steadfast counsel and example the author was seeking to reinforce by this powerful "word of exhortation" (verse 17). What they needed above all to develop was that total response to God's will so wonderfully exemplified by the Lord himself in submitting to death – death which brought them, by bringing first to him, access into the eternal realm to which the Law could never bring them.

"Now the God of peace [prayed the author], that brought again from the dead our Lord Jesus, that great shepherd of the sheep, through the blood of the everlasting covenant, make you perfect in every good work to do his will, working in you that which is well-pleasing in his sight, through Jesus Christ; to whom be glory for ever and ever. Amen." (verses 20,21)

## The modern situation

The time has been long, the changes many, since that prayer was penned, and great though the differences were between the situation in which these Hebrew Christians found themselves and that of other Christians – whether Jewish or non-Jewish – in, say, Ephesus, Corinth, or even Rome, at the time, the differences between their situation and that of us Gentiles in these days are of necessity greater still.

Much, for example, that was axiomatic for them – the existence of God, the inspiration and authority of Scripture, the divine control of human history – is challenged and even denied today. The plain fact is that were both the writer and the readers of Hebrews to come alive in our day, and recommence their Christian career in our contemporary world, many of their problems and their needs – and so the form and content of any letter composed to meet those problems and those needs – would be altogether different from those with which this study of Hebrews has made us so familiar.

Since the world is constantly changing, a purely static attitude to it is neither possible nor wise. Each age brings its challenge, and, to be successfully met, that challenge needs first to be recognized for what it is. To blind one's eye to that fact is simply to repeat the error of these Hebrews and, like them, to be caught unawares when the storm of difficulty bursts upon us.

## Unchanging human nature

Yet in history, ever changing though it be, there are certain constants. That is assuredly one of the great lessons which Hebrews teaches us – as it taught the first readers. Chief among those constants on the human side is, alas, human nature itself, with the result that certain problems recur automatically in every age – that of loss of faith, of loss of enthusiasm, of undue concern with immediate short term benefits which in the long run prove destructive of true spiritual life. Whatever, in fact, may be the particular situation in which any one Christian either practises, or betrays, his Christian principles, his reactions to it conform to a clearly defined pattern.

## The parable of the Sower

The Gospel inevitably, as Jesus taught in the parable of the Sower, sorts men out into groups. Of these the largest of all is made up of those who reject the Gospel outright – those by the wayside, that "hear" but in whose case there at once "cometh the devil, and taketh away the word out of their hearts, lest they should believe and be saved" (Luke 8:12). Over against these, however, stands the whole company of Christians – those who hear, and who, hearing, also believe. But for them, believing is not the end: it is only the beginning and within this group, as a whole, experience unfailingly creates subdivisions.

There are, unhappily, those which "have no root, which for a while believe, and in time of temptation fall away"; those who "endure but for a time" – who, "when affliction or persecution ariseth for the word's sake immediately are offended" (Luke 8:13; Mark 4:17). The sad thing about this group of Christians is that they in the first place accept the Gospel with enthusiasm – "with joy", as Luke puts it; or, as Mark has it, "with gladness". But they lack spiritual stamina; and with as great an alacrity as they accept the Gospel they also renounce it.

With others the case is even more tragic. For it is not for want of vigour that they fail: it is solely because that vigour is misdirected. It spends itself not only on the Gospel but also on those things which are destructive of it. The good seed and the worthless weed both grow together – but in soil, alas, which is more congenial to the development of the latter than of the former. So steadily but remorselessly –

> "the cares of this world, and the deceitfulness of riches, and the lusts of other things entering in, choke the word, and it becometh unfruitful."
>
> (Mark 4:19)

There we have depicted the tragedy of a lifetime spent in discipleship with nothing by way of spiritual fruit to show for it in the end – a purely futile probation.

What proportion of men thus reject the Gospel outright or embrace it simply to forsake it in the hour of trial or to frustrate its operation in themselves, is not indicated in the parable. It is clearly a proportion which varies from age to age. Yet whether it be great or small, in each age, happily, there remains also a faithful band of Christians who, each to varying degrees, bear fruit for God. They are the counterpart of the seed sown in good ground – such as "hear" the word, like all others; who then "receive" it as do even those other Christians who fall short of their calling; but who also go on thereafter to "bring forth fruit", some thirtyfold, some sixty, and some an hundred (verse 20).

It was to this latter group that the writer of Hebrews wished each of his readers to belong, and hoped that his letter would help them to belong. "We desire", said he, "that every one of you do show the same diligence to the full assurance of hope unto the end". To begin, said he, in effect, is not enough: nor is to continue in a spirit of half-heartedness a whit the better; what is needed is resolute persistence until the goal of discipleship is reached.

"LET US GO FORTH THEREFORE UNTO HIM"

## The goal of discipleship

For discipleship assuredly *has* a goal, that goal being the great constant on the divine side, a constant of which men of every age should take account, and with an eye to which they should shape their lives. Within Hebrews itself that goal receives a whole variety of definitions – among other things, it is spoken of as inclusion in God's House; entry into His Rest; the receiving of a promised eternal inheritance; attainment to a heavenly country. But however it be conceived – and that depends largely on each individual's needs and circumstances – the important thing is that it is a *fact* – an ultimate reality. Life, that is, has a purpose which extends beyond the present, a purpose sure of realization if life is lived faithfully in Christ:

"We are made partakers of Christ, if we hold the beginning of our confidence stedfast unto the end."

(Hebrews 3:14)

Though, therefore, the author was addressing himself to his readers specifically in terms of their own preoccupations at the time, when he told them, "Here have we no continuing city but we seek one to come", he was in the process expressing a principle which holds good in every age of waiting for Christ's coming. What he meant was that not now, but only hereafter, can life's goal be attained, and that the living of life must be adjusted to that fundamental fact. Short cuts to glory there are none: the Son of God himself was made perfect through sufferings; so, therefore, must his followers be in their turn.

The form in which the Lord himself expressed that truth was that "the disciple is not above his master, nor the servant above his lord". "It is enough", said he, "that the disciple be as his master, and the servant as his lord" (Matthew 10:24,25). The truth as such was here, of course, couched in general terms, but it was intended, on the occasion which Matthew records, to apply to a particular experience. The Lord was commissioning his apostles. Their duty would be to witness for him. But the discouragements would in their case be many – and great. Among them would be the greatest discouragement of all – the suffering of death itself.

"But [said Jesus, paradoxically] he that endureth to the end shall be saved." (verses 21,22)

At the time this would appear to be more of a promise than a guarantee, for Jesus himself had yet to prove it true in his own experience. He had, however, no hesitation in offering it to them as a guarantee, because he knew that death would not have dominion over him – that he would die not as an exemplar merely, but, instead, as a Saviour, to rise thereafter to power and glory, to appear on his apostles' behalf in the presence of God Himself. And by the time, indeed, that those same apostles were themselves brought face to face with this dire experience, his confidence had vindicated itself utterly – he was alive for evermore and had power over death and hell, power committed to him by God. His words, because of his own resurrection, had thus by then acquired additional – and irresistible – power to encourage.

## The fact of the resurrection

Now it was that fact – that new constant – which the writer to the Hebrews made the ground of his confidence and the starting point of his exhortations. "We behold Jesus", said he, "crowned with glory and honour". His readers had therefore to reckon with that fact in their present predicament. What if they were called upon by their unbelieving brethren to recant – to declare that Jesus was *not* the Son of God, that his death was devoid of sacrificial potency, that the miracles wrought by him and his were after all wrought with the power of Beelzebub? (cf. p.69). Their denials – if they in craven fear of death should prove guilty of them – would not and could not alter the facts. True, those denials would bring them relief from immediate suffering – but only to involve them in suffering far more terrible later! Conversely their steadfastness, even if it cost them the

## "LET US GO FORTH THEREFORE UNTO HIM"

extreme penalty at the time, would make their ultimate deliverance certain.

Such had been precisely the truth communicated by Jesus to his apostles:

> "Fear them not therefore [he had said] ... What I tell you in darkness, that speak ye in light: and what ye hear in the ear, that preach ye upon the housetops. And fear not them which kill the body, but are not able to kill the soul: but rather fear him which is able to destroy both soul and body in Gehenna."
> (Matthew 10:26-28)

To encourage them he disclosed that God takes note of the death of the meanest creature – such as the common sparrow. Would *their* death go unnoticed by Him, then? Assuredly not. "The very hairs of your head [said he] are all numbered. Fear ye not therefore [he added], ye are of more value than many sparrows" (see verses 29-31).

### False sense of security

Today, as we read these words in the Gospel, or others to the same effect in Hebrews, we may well wonder where their pertinence lies for us. Of all the changes wrought by time, none is more remarkable than our modern freedom to lead a quiet and peaceable life in all godliness and honesty. "Fear them not", seems unnecessary counsel today, as the Christian, like his unbelieving fellow-citizens, benefits from the State's defence of his right of free speech.

But let us not be lulled by our present privileges into a sense of false security, as were the Hebrews, by a whole generation of comfortable compromise. For we, like them, live under an order doomed to dissolution. As the ruin of Jerusalem, and, with it, the removal of the whole polity of Jewry amid fire and blood was imminent when Hebrews was written, so is the fulfilment of Haggai's forecast of the shaking of all nations virtually upon us. The great powers jockey for positions of advantage in readiness for a conflict which they would fain avoid but which, ironically, their very own policies render inevitable. Behind the talk of peace proceeds the same devilishly thorough preparation for war as all past history has witnessed. Thus, having regard to the dread totality of the struggle when it comes, a blind confidence in the fact that this land will escape the horrors of military occupation might well prove a snare and delusion. Any, or all, of us may yet be faced with an ultimatum from those whose ideology makes them sworn enemies of all religion, and who are bent on its extirpation, to cease our witness. Should that occur how then should we stand? Would we defy the ban? Or, knowing the consequences of defiance to be death, would we tamely submit? In such a crisis we, like the apostles, would need all the encouragement that could be wrung from the Master's words – "Fear them not. What I tell you in darkness, that speak ye upon the housetops". We might even be confronted, as were the Hebrews, with an actual demand to recant and declare our faith in Christ a futile superstition – or to accept death, whether swift or lingering, as the penalty of refusal. In such an event what new weight and force the words of Jesus would suddenly acquire for us:

"Whosoever shall confess me before men, him will I confess also before my Father which is in heaven."

And the same would be true of those other words of omen which went with them:

"But whosoever shall deny me before men, him will I also deny before my Father which is in heaven."

(Matthew 10:32,33)

Of course it may yet be that no such crisis will befall us. But if not that, then some other. For conflict there will most assuredly be: and as ideology contends with ideology the battle cry will, as always, be, "Liberty versus tyranny". Our sympathy with the cause of "liberty" will, we can be sure, be fiercely canvassed, and subtle propaganda, forgetful of the horror and injustice and indiscriminate slaughter of modern war, will seek to make out that cause to be so noble, so just, so worthy of our active support. If we be true to our faith, however – true to the counsel of Hebrews – we shall not be blinded by the dust of mere words to the rottenness of our modern democracy with its by-products of moral licence, cultural decadence, political sharp practice, and idolatrous concern with "the meat which perisheth".

**Certainty of Christ's coming**

There is but One fit, and able, to exercise dominion – he whose right it is. His Coming, however long delayed, is the great certainty of future history. It was in fulfilment of the ancient ritual that he went in beyond the veil: and it will again be in fulfilment of it that he will in due course appear the second time upon this sin-stricken earth. In expectation of that Coming we, like Abraham and like the Hebrews in Palestine, must also in our turn confess ourselves strangers and pilgrims in whatever land happens to serve us as an earthly home. Of us, as of them, it is true to say, "Here have we no continuing city, but we seek one to come".

The only attitude consistent with such a faith is one of political neutrality. However good any one political system may appear to us to be, the fact is that it is "good" only in the degree to which it is less evil than some other which strives with it for the mastery. And the fact to be faced is that both will one day have to make way for a better, when, in the person of the all-powerful Son of God, the holy city, the new Jerusalem, will come down from God out of heaven, and in the earth at large, and not in the Promised Land only, the time will have come for the establishment of a new heaven and a new earth. Then will be heard a great voice out of heaven saying:

"Behold, the tabernacle of God is with men, and he will dwell with them, and they shall be his people, and God himself shall be with them, and be their God. And God shall wipe away all tears from their eyes; and there shall be no more death, neither sorrow, nor crying, neither shall there be any more pain: for the former things are passed away."

(Revelation 21:3,4)

## Separation from the world

We must, then, go out of the Camp of our modern civilization, Christianized though it be in some measure, and make our way as social and spiritual pilgrims toward the Rest which awaits us.

But does that mean a separation from the world so complete that our Christianity has no opportunity – or urge – to prove itself in the world? No: that would be tragedy. Virtue lies not in shunning or denouncing the world only, but in contending actively against it, and seeking to transform it, by example as well as precept. As the Lord himself declared to the Father:

"I pray not that thou shouldest take them out of the world, but that thou shouldest keep them from the evil. They [said he, of his disciples] are not of the world, even as I am not of the world."

But he also added:

"Sanctify them through thy truth: thy word is truth. As thou hast sent me into the world, *even so have I also sent them into the world.*" (John 17:15-18)

His own coming into the world was entire: he moved amongst the worst of men – refining them without himself being coarsened. In this, as in all things, he was our exemplar, and in sending us, in our turn, into the world he has delegated the same task to us. While therefore it is as timely as ever to renew the call, "Let us go forth unto him", it is equally timely to remind ourselves – "And to do good forget not". We are in the world to do good in it and to it. The light we cast amidst its gloom must be not only doctrinal, but ethical. That our word might have power it is essential that the conformity of our own lives to it should be manifest:

"Let your light [said Jesus] so shine before men, that they may see your good works, and glorify your Father which is in heaven." (Matthew 5:16)

## Tomorrow is too late

The time to do this is now. The Scripture is still valid – *"Today* – if ye will hear his voice". Tomorrow spells judgement, with its start alternative – either life eternal with glory everlasting, or death eternal in shame and everlasting contempt. "Behold, now is the accepted time; behold, now is the day of salvation". We neglect any opportunity of spiritual development to our peril. It would be to our abiding shame and loss if, with signs so portentous about us, a crisis befell us for which we could have prepared ourselves but did not – be it from lack of zeal for the cause of Christ, or from fear of unsettling ourselves from a pleasant routine merely because it was so congenial to us. We, too, everyone, have weights which hinder us, some sin which so easily besets us, as had the Hebrews. But, like them, we have also a race to run – a race which can be successfully run only if we put those hindrances away and run it with "patience", that resolution which enabled Jesus, the author and finisher of our faith, to endure the Cross, despising the shame, and thereafter to sit down at the right hand of the throne of God.

**A new and living way**

There, in the Holiest, he still remains as yet. But he ministers there on our behalf, no less than of old on behalf of those Hebrews. He is touched with the feeling of our infirmities as of theirs – and is ready to succour us as he was to succour them. It is therefore for us in our turn to avail ourselves of his help. True, the issues which so seriously – and almost tragically – exercised them, now belong to a past age, but the liturgical language, in which the epistle's words of encouragement and warning were couched, still speaks powerfully and clearly to us. It is the testimony of "the Holy Spirit" as much as was the ancient ritual upon which it is so powerful a commentary, and must by us be heeded as such as we await the re-appearing of our High Priest. Let us therefore appropriate to ourselves the counsel of the Spirit:

"Having therefore, brethren, boldness to enter into the holiest by the blood of Jesus, by a new and living way, which he hath consecrated for us, through the veil, that is to say, his flesh; and having an high priest over the house of God; let us draw near with a true heart in full assurance of faith, having our hearts sprinkled from an evil conscience, and our bodies washed with pure water. Let us hold fast the profession of our faith without wavering; (for he is faithful that promised;) and let us consider one another to provoke unto love and to good works: not forsaking the assembling of ourselves together, as the manner of some is; but exhorting one another: and so much the more, as ye see the day approaching."

(Hebrews 10:19-25)

Thus the epistle reminds us that Christ died for us – and now appears before God for us – not only individually but also collectively. We are each components of God's House: none of us can neglect his own spiritual wellbeing without in the same measure impairing that of the Household of Faith as a whole; nor, conversely, can he dissociate himself from its corporate life and worship without involving himself in loss and danger. Our spiritual life is a fragile growth: it needs most careful fostering – by the closest fellowship with God in Christ, and by the closest fellowship with one another as fellow pilgrims Zionwards. Please God that our joint study of this portion of His Word will have helped to make such fellowship more real for us all, so that when he that shall come will come, he shall see in us of the travail of his soul – and shall be *satisfied*.

# SCRIPTURE REFERENCE INDEX

**Genesis**
1:1-3 ..................... 55
:26 ........................ 73
:27,28 ................... 73
**12**:2 ...................... 123
**15**:5 ...................... 124
:6 ......................... 124
:8-18 .................... 39
**22**:2 ...................... 124
:11,12 ................. 125
:16-18 ............... 125
**Exodus**
4:8 ........................ 37
:22 ....................... 132
**20**:19 .................... 139
**33**:18,19 ................ 54
**34**:5-7 .................... 54
**Leviticus**
1:9 ....................... 136
**4**:1-21 ................. 137
:1-22 ................. 104
:4 ......................... 104
:7,18 .................. 101
**6**:24-29 .............. 136
:30 ....................... 137
**8**:1-14 .................. 85
**11**:32 .................... 102
**16**:4,20-28 .......... 101
:4,23,24 ............ 106
:15-19 ............... 108
:16,21 ............... 106
:27 ....................... 137
:30-34 ................. 98
:33 ....................... 108
**17**:11 .... 102, 104, 107
**21**:1-12 ................. 87
:16-21 ................. 86

**23**:28-30 ............... 98
**Numbers**
**13**:33 ...................... 64
**14**:2 ........................ 33
:24 ........................ 34
:25 ........................ 34
:40-45 ................. 64
**19**:15 .................... 102
**31**:28-30 ............... 33
**Deuteronomy**
**5**:23,29 ............... 139
**8**:2,3 ................... 132
:5 ......................... 132
**17**:2-7 .................... 70
**2 Samuel**
**7**:14 ........................ 49
**Psalms**
**2**: ............................. 48
:7 .......................... 89
**8**: ...................... 72, 97
:3-5 ..................... 74
:6 .......................... 74
**22**:22 ...................... 28
**33**:6,9 .................... 55
**40**:6-8 ................... 28
**95**: ............................ 11
:7-11 .................. 31
**102**: ........................ 51
:25-27 .......... 50, 53
:26,27 ................. 52
**110**:1 ...................... 94
:4 36, 94, 115, 126
**Isaiah**
**8**:17,18 .................. 28
**35**:2-4 ................... 134
**53**: ........................... 80
**65**:17 ..................... 52

**Jeremiah**
**31**:31 ...................... 11
:31-34 ..... 114, 115, 116
**Haggai**
**2**:6,7 ..................... 120
:7 ......................... 120
**Malachi**
**1**:7 ....................... 136
**Matthew**
**5**:16 ...................... 150
**10**:21,22 ............... 146
:24,25 ............... 145
:26-28 ............. 147
:29-31 ............. 147
:32,33 ............... 148
**12**:24-32 ................ 70
**Mark**
**4**:17 ...................... 143
:19 ....................... 144
:20 ....................... 144
**Luke**
**8**:12 ...................... 143
:13 ....................... 143
**John**
**17**:15-18 ............ 150
**Acts**
**3**:25,26 .................. 65
**6**:–7: ....................... 9
**7**:53 ....................... 46
**10**:–11: .................... 9
**15**: ........................... 10
**1 Corinthians**
**9**:13 ...................... 136
:24-27 ................. 10
**10**:1-12 .................. 10
:14-20 ............... 136

153

## THE LETTER TO THE HEBREWS

**Hebrews**

**1**:1.........................35
:1,2.. 32, 54, 58, 96
:1-4 ....................47
:1,39......................11
:2...........52, 55, 112
:2,3......................76
:2,5......................55
:2,13....................55
:3..... 29, 54, 55, 71
:4........................47
:5........................45
:6........................49
:7,8......................49
:9........................49
:10......................59
:10-12 ...........51, 55
:11,12..................40
:12......................53
:13  45, 51, 76, 119
:14................51, 53
**2**:1............45, 46, 58
:1-4 ..............50, 51
:2........................45
:2,3......................59
:3...............6, 41, 46
:3,4......................59
:4............5, 32, 112
:5........................53
:5-18 .............51, 60
:6-10 ...................55
:7,8......................75
:8.................64, 75
:9................78, 108
:9,10....................42
:9-17 ...................59
:10................54, 78
:11.......................79
:11-13 .................28
:12,13..................79
:14.......................79
:16.................11, 79
:17..........11, 13, 82
:17,18...........81, 97
**3**:1..................41, 82
:1-6 ....................27

:2-6 ....................56
:3........................56
:4........................54
:5........................60
:6................43, 56
:6 to **4**:11 ...........31
:6-11 ...................31
:7,8...................113
:9.........................11
:12......................32
:12,13.................67
:13......................32
:14..........6, 33, 145
:15......................33
:16-19 .................33
:17................32, 61
:17-19 .................34
**4**:1,2.....................34
:3-7 .....................34
:3-8 .....................16
:7..........................36
:8..........................36
:8-10 ...................35
:9..........................34
:10,11................123
:11........................35
:12,13..................82
:14................83, 97
:15.......................42
:15,16..................83
**5**:1.........................84
:1-3 .....................84
:1-5 .....................27
:2..........................84
:3................13, 86
:4..........................84
:4-6 .....................88
:7..........................29
:7,8..............42, 89
:9............42, 91, 94
:9,10.............89, 91
:10................62, 91
:11.......................65
:11,12..................92
:12.................63, 65
:12-14 ............6, 62

:14........................63
**6**:1.........................65
:1,3......................63
:2..........................65
:3-6 .....................63
:4-6 ..............64, 66
:5..........................41
:7,8......................66
:8..........................41
:9,10..................123
:11..............62, 123
:11,12........62, 123
:12-14 ..............126
:16,17..................41
:17......................30
:17,18...............126
:18.......................21
:18-20 .................97
:19.......................41
:19,20..................91
:20.........29, 62, 126
**7**:1-3 .....................92
:4-10 ...................93
:5..........................13
:8..........................92
:11.......................36
:11,12...............115
:12.......................53
:14.......................29
:15-17 .................93
:16,17...............117
:18,19...............115
:19................27, 93
:20-22 ......116, 117
:21....................126
:22...............37, 41
:23........................94
:23,24..................96
:24........................94
:24,25...............108
:25................41, 94
:26........................94
:26,27..................97
:27....................110
:28..........29, 36, 95
**8**:.........................59

154

## SCRIPTURE REFERENCE INDEX

:1......................100
:2......................100
:3......................100
:4..........23, 91, 100
:5......................100
:6..........27, 53, 100
:8......................113
:8-13 ..................11
:9......................113
:10-12 ...............114
:13..........23, 37, 52
**9**:2,6..................102
:5..........................4
:6......................101
:7......................102
:8.............102, 113
:9........................90
:9,10..................103
:10................26, 52
:11........................27
:11,12................103
:13,14................107
:14...........108, 116
:14,15..................65
:15........37, 59, 116
:15-17 ..............108
:16,17.........38, 119
:17........................39
:18........................39
:20........................37
:22........................39
:23..................27, 41
:23,24..........55, 109
:24........29, 42, 109
:25,26...............109
:26.............52, 109
:27,28.........64, 110
:28....................111
**10**:1......................29
:1,2...................117
:1-3 .....................99
:1,14....................90
:3......................117
:4......................118

:5-7 ..................118
:5-11 ..................28
:8,9...................119
:10....................119
:11-13 ..............119
:14-17 ..............120
:15-17 ..............113
:18....................120
:19,20................42
:19-25 ..............152
:22-24 ................68
:23........................41
:25........................68
:26,27..................69
:28,29..................69
:29..........................6
:30,31................70
:32..........................6
:32-34 ..............127
:32-37 ................70
:34........................25
:35,36..............127
:35-37 ................30
:36........................41
:38........................70
:39..............70, 128
**11**:1......................41
:3..................41, 54
:6..................22, 25
:8........................17
:9........................18
:10........................20
:15,16..................20
:16........................20
:17-19 ..............129
:24-27 ................19
:26....................141
:26,27..............129
:27........................41
:32-40 ................41
:35-38 ................24
:39,40..............130
:40........................90
:51........................25

**12**:1-3 ..............6, 131
:5,6...................132
:9......................133
:10....................133
:11,12...............133
:12-17 ................42
:13-17 ..............134
:16........................25
:16,17..................64
:18-24 ..............134
:19,25...............139
:22........................22
:23................70, 90
:24........................52
:25................32, 56
:25-27 ................23
:26.............52, 120
:27........................40
:28........................40
:28,29.........23, 121
:29........................43
**13**:1-5 ....................43
:7,8......................40
:7,17....................21
:8........................52
:9.........41, 47, 138
:9-15 .....................7
:10....................138
:11....................138
:12.............29, 140
:13,14.........20, 141
:14........................22
:15....................141
:16....................141
:17....................141
:20........................29
:20,21................142
:22....................1, 4
:39........................21
**2 Peter**
**3**:10-13 ................52
**Revelation**
**21**:3,4..................149

155

## OTHER BOOKS BY THE AUTHOR

THE book *Law and Grace*, first published in 1952, is based on a set of full-length lecture notes. These were compiled for use with a course of twelve addresses on the Law of Moses which the author delivered in the autumn of 1951 to a Bible Study Class in Central London. It is described by the author as "A devotional study of the Law of Moses – the Mosaic ordinances viewed as an education in acceptable worship and a discipline in holy living".

Although, as he suggests, the subject is capable of expansion into a much fuller and more detailed study, the author hopes that the book will provide readers with the key to understanding the Law as a whole and be an inducement to further examination of its precepts.

The hardback edition has 208 pages and includes indexes of Scripure references and subjects. It is still in print and available from the publisher.

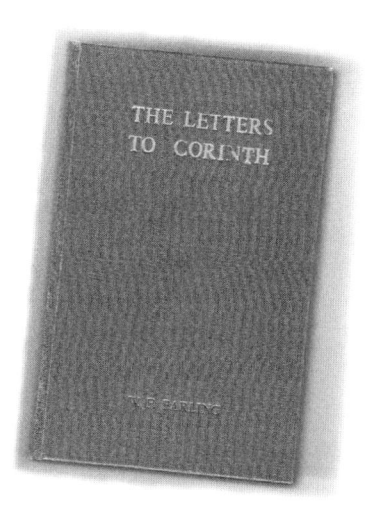

IN common with the current volume on Hebrews, *Law and Grace*, and *Jesus – Healer and Teacher*, this book is a revised and expanded version of full-length lecture notes recording the substance of a series of addresses delivered to a Bible Study Class in Central London in the 1950s.

It aims to give the meaning that the letters to the Corinthian Ecclesia had for those who were the first to read them.

This endeavour has inevitably entailed dealing with problems of background, but this has been kept to a minimum on account of the intrinsic difficulty of the study of two works as lengthy and as complex as the two letters to the Corinthians.

The result is designed to be read as a normal book, and to that extent different from most commentaries. It goes without saying, however, that it is meant to be used only in close conjunction with the epistles themselves.

The 1974 hardback edition (red cover) has 250 pages including a Scripture index. It is out of print, but used copies are available from time to time.

DESCRIBED as "A discursive study of the ministry of our Lord based on the Synoptic Gospels", this book also began life as notes to accompany twelve lectures presented to a Bible Class in Central London. In this case, the year was 1952.

"Discursive" is used in the sense of going from premise to conclusion in a series of logical steps. The progression from the first apparently audacious claims to be the Messiah, to the dying breath upon the cross, is faithfully followed.

Jesus is shown to be the centre of all things from the first to the last – the Alpha and the Omega. Although the journey is suspended at the crucifixion, the fact of the resurrection is implied throughout as the driving force behind the Gospel records.

Here Jesus is shown elevated as supreme Lord and Master over his disciples, and the one with ultimate power over his enemies. We are caused to think searchingly of our own relationship with the Master and the practical outworking of Christ's teaching in our lives.

The current paperback edition has 304 pages and is available from the publisher.